Regain Health and Energy!

Living in a World of Unhealthy Food

JOANNA LOKS

Author: Joanna Loks

Publisher: NEW SEVEN LTD

Address: 590 Kingston Road, London, England, SW20 8DN

ISBN: 978-3-1240-0893-0 (Paperback)
978-3-1740-0140-0 (Hardcover)
978-3-5240-2002-0 (E-book)

ACKNOWLEDGMENTS

I would like to express my immense gratitude to my partner, Tom. Without his unwavering support, I would not be where I am today, and this book would never have been written. I dedicate it to him, thanking him for his invaluable help and support in finding a new, healthier life.

I also want to thank my mother, Ela, for her warmth and support during difficult times.

It is thanks to them that I was able to fully immerse myself in the process of healing and transformation.

Table of Contents

INTRODUCTION

In Search of Health in Today's World

Hello, Dear Reader,

We live in an era dominated by modern technologies and constant progress, yet our health often stands at a crossroads. The everyday decisions we make while shopping can significantly impact our lives. Have you ever wondered what lies behind those colorful packages and eye-catching health promises? Do you know how much what you put into your shopping cart affects your health, well-being, and longevity?

Every journey begins with a single step. My journey to a healthy lifestyle started ten years ago when I faced serious health issues. I was constantly tired, had severe digestive and women's health problems, joint pains, and my immunity was very weak. I had no energy for anything, and depressive states began to appear. Visits to doctors usually ended with a long list of medications I was supposed to take. I was offered various pharmaceutical solutions to alleviate my ailments, but I felt they only masked the symptoms and did not address the root causes of my problems. I felt that this approach wouldn't work and that something needed to change.

During this difficult period, I met my partner, who instilled in me the desire for change and introduced me to natural healing methods. His support and search for alternative treatments were a window to a better life for me. Thanks to him, I became more interested in natural remedies, diet therapy, and a holistic approach to health.

In the face of feeling unwell, I began by making dietary changes, eliminating processed foods, gluten, casein, and sugar, and incorporating more healthy fats, vegetables, and fruits, especially berries rich in antioxidants. I started drinking high-quality water, about 2-3 liters a day. Over time, I noticed an improvement in my well-being and an increase in energy levels. This encouraged me to further explore topics related to healthy eating and lifestyle choices.

It wasn't easy. There were moments of doubt and difficulties, but gradually I discovered how powerful our daily choices are for our health. Education became my key to health—I started reading, attending workshops and courses, consulting with experts, and after completing a four-year program, I delved into the intricacies of medicine, dietetics, homotoxicology, the fundamentals of psychology, homeopathy, naturopathy, and the holistic approach to our bodies. I became a homeopath. I came to understand that health is not just the absence of disease but a complete physical, mental, and social well-being.

My personal journey inspired me to write this book. I want to share with you the knowledge and experiences I've gained over the years. Through education and conscious choices, we can improve the quality of our lives and health.

I hope this book will be a source of inspiration and support for you on your path to a healthy lifestyle.

"Regain Health and Energy! Living in a World of Unhealthy Food." is a guide that will unveil the complex world of modern food, its hidden dangers, and potential solutions. We will discuss the impact of gluten, casein, sugar, trans fats, GMO foods, pesticides, and herbicides that end up on our plates, and show how to protect ourselves from them.

This book aims not only to provide you with knowledge but also to inspire and motivate you to make changes that will benefit your health. You will find numerous tips for gluten-free, casein-free, and sugar-free dishes that are not only healthy but also delicious. These dishes have been staples in my kitchen for years. I want you to feel equipped with the necessary tools to understand the importance of what is on your plate and how conscious decisions can transform your life.

Our Body as a Home and Vehicle

I would like to illustrate the functioning of our body in a clear and visual way. Comparing our body to a home and a vehicle that we take care of can help us better understand the importance of maintaining health and daily habits.

Our body is our home, where we live, and the vehicle that we use to move around.

Every day, we take care of our home: we clean, wash windows, mop floors, paint, buy new furniture, beautify the garden, mow the lawn, and water the flowers. For our car, we regularly conduct check-ups, service it, change the oil, fill it with good fuel, and replace filters and tires when necessary. What about our body? It also needs good fuel—minerals, vitamins, and micro and macro elements—to function efficiently, to "drive." It needs water so it doesn't wither like grass, and good "oil" so all systems operate correctly. Just as a house needs occasional deep cleaning and a car requires an annual service, our body needs regular detoxification and healthy daily nutrition.

This book is an invitation to a journey. It may not be an easy road, but I promise it will be incredibly rewarding. Together, we will uncover the true picture of the world we live in and discover, step by step, how we can make our lives healthier and more fulfilling. Additionally, I will share with you tips and products that I use in my own life.

This book is for you.

I believe that with each chapter you read, you will discover new ways to take care of your health and well-being.

I invite you to begin this journey. Together, we will delve into the topics of health and nutrition, and in the end, find the key to a long and healthy life.

Thank you for choosing to embark on this journey toward a healthier, more conscious life. Your health is in your hands, and every small step you take has tremendous significance. I hope you find in this book not only information but also motivation and support on your path.

I wish You health, happiness, and success in every aspect of your life. Remember, each day is a new opportunity to make positive changes. This book is for you—to help you enjoy life fully and mindfully.

With gratitude,
Joanna

PART I

MODERN NUTRITIONAL CHALLENGES

CHAPTER 1

Understanding Contamination - What's Hidden in Our Food?

Entering a supermarket, we encounter an abundance of food products wrapped in colorful packaging that promise health and taste. Behind these eye-catching slogans often lie substances that can have significant consequences for our health. We rarely consider the actual composition of what we are about to consume. Modern food is often saturated with various additives—from preservatives to artificial colorings.

Discovering and realizing that we live in times where I must be cautious about the products I buy in the store was a huge surprise for me. Just a few decades ago, people didn't worry about what they ate because food wasn't modified, and the world wasn't so polluted. Food provided everything our bodies needed to function healthily.

Today, however, global development has gone in the wrong direction, and our food is often loaded with chemicals that can pose potential threats to our health and well-being. Pharmaceutical companies make billions from our health, selling medications that are supposed to counteract diseases resulting from poor diet and environmental pollutants, which do not necessarily improve our health. This highlights the importance of making conscious decisions about our nutrition and lifestyle.

Hippocrates, the Greek physician known as the "father of medicine," advised: "Let food be your medicine, and medicine be your food." His message holds deep wisdom—proper nutrition is the key to health and well-being. In today's complex world, full of processed foods and pollutants, we must understand that food can be both our greatest ally and a potential threat. Properly selected nutrients can act like medicine, supporting our health on many levels, whereas poor dietary choices can lead to various health problems.

What Are "Toxins" in Food?

Let's start by explaining what science recognizes as toxins. These are substances that can be harmful to our bodies in certain quantities. Our daily diet can contain many examples of such substances. Processed meats often contain preservatives like nitrates, which can convert into nitrosamines in the body, compounds with potentially carcinogenic properties. Soft drinks and fast food are filled with artificial additives that enhance the taste and appearance of the product but can also negatively impact health.

We encounter a wide range of artificial toxins added during food processing, including preservatives, colorings, and flavor enhancers. While these improve the aesthetics and taste of products, they can simultaneously pose a threat to our health.

Main Sources of Toxins in Our Diet

Among the main sources of toxins in our diet are pesticides and herbicides used in agriculture, which often remain on vegetables and fruits. Various food additives and heavy metals, such as lead, mercury, cadmium, and arsenic, can enter food from contaminated water and soil, becoming a significant threat. Commonly consumed bread and dairy products can also be potential sources of herbicides and antibiotics.

Consequences of Consuming Toxins

Consuming toxins is often unavoidable, but it is associated with various health risks. In the short term, they can cause allergic reactions, headaches, and fatigue, while long-term exposure can lead to chronic inflammation. This increases the risk of more serious conditions such as heart disease, type 2 diabetes, and various forms of cancer.

How to Protect Yourself from Toxins

There is good news—we can make conscious decisions to minimize our exposure to these toxins. Reading product labels and avoiding foods with long lists of unknown ingredients is one way to protect ourselves. Choosing organic products free from artificial additives and grown without the use of harmful chemicals is another step toward a healthier diet. Supporting local farmers and preferring fresh, seasonal products also helps reduce the amount of toxins we encounter daily.

Understanding the composition of our food is fundamental to protecting our health. By making informed dietary choices, we can significantly reduce the risk of adverse health effects and enjoy a longer, fuller life. Additionally, we can support our body's detoxification processes, helping it manage the inevitable excess of toxic substances that affect our well-being and health in today's world.

However, this is just the beginning of our journey. In the following chapters, we will delve deeper into the impact of specific ingredients on our bodies and how to wisely manage our diet to ensure the best health for ourselves and our loved ones.

Understanding what is hidden in our food is the first step toward protecting our health and improving our quality of life. I encourage everyone to delve deeper into this topic to make more informed choices every day.

Each chapter will gradually reveal new, valuable information, allowing for a deeper understanding of the impact of food on our lives and health. This will help ensure health and well-being for ourselves and our loved ones for years to come.

PART II

NUTRIENTS AND THEIR IMPACT

CHAPTER 2

The Sweet Trap - The Invisible Danger of Sugar

Few of us can resist the sweet taste of sugar, which is ubiquitous in many aspects of our daily diet. From coffee to snacks to full meals, sugar is added to almost everything, often hiding under various names, making it difficult to avoid. What many of us consider a source of pleasure can also become a health trap, one that we may fall into without even realizing it.

Sugar is not only a source of empty calories with no nutritional value, but its excessive consumption is strongly linked to many serious health problems, such as obesity, type 2 diabetes, heart disease, digestive issues, tooth decay, and many other ailments. Why, then, do our bodies crave something that can harm them, and how can we break free from this sweet trap?

The Biology of Sugar Cravings

Understanding why we love sugar so much requires a look at our biology. Sugar stimulates the release of serotonin, a neurotransmitter that improves mood and makes us feel happy. This reward mechanism evolved to encourage our ancestors to consume sweet, energy-rich foods, which made sense in times when food was scarce. Today, with easy access to food, this ancient instinct still drives us, leading to excessive sugar consumption.

Sugar: How It Affects Our Body

Sugar, a ubiquitous ingredient in our daily diet, plays a significant role in the functioning of the human body. Its impact is extensive, from the immediate supply of energy to more complex, long-term health effects.

Sugar is a fundamental source of energy for the cells of the human body. Glucose, the simplest form of sugar, is essential for the functioning of the brain, muscles, and other key biological processes. After consumption, simple sugars are quickly absorbed by the body, leading to an immediate increase in blood glucose levels, providing the energy needed for functioning. However, this energy is quickly used up, prompting us to reach for another dose of sugar. In an era of sedentary lifestyles and lack of physical activity, consuming sugar in excess is associated with serious health consequences.

Everyday Products and Sugar

Sugar is found almost everywhere, hidden in the products we consume daily, often in surprisingly large amounts. Let's imagine a typical day: starting with a slice of bread, followed by yogurt as a snack, then cake for dessert, and the beverages we drink. Each of these products can contain sugar, and the total amount often significantly exceeds the recommended limits.

- **Bread:**
  Even in traditional bakery bread, which seems neutral, you can find about 1 to 2 grams of sugar per slice. Choosing sweetened

types of bread, like those with added honey or raisins, can significantly increase the sugar content.

- **Yogurts:**
  Natural yogurt is usually a healthy choice, but even some "natural" yogurts contain added sugar. Fruit or flavored yogurts can contain as much as 20-30 grams of sugar per serving, which is nearly the entire recommended daily intake of sugar.

- **Cakes and Cookies:**
  Sweet snacks are notoriously high in sugar, with some cakes and cookies containing as much as 40-60 grams of sugar per serving, which exceeds the daily recommendation.

- **Soft Drinks and Juices:**
  Beverages are one of the biggest sources of sugar in many people's diets. A typical can of soda can contain about 35-40 grams of sugar, while boxed fruit juices, even those advertised as "100% juice," can have similar amounts of sugar per serving.

Daily Sugar Intake

Health organizations, such as the World Health Organization, recommend that added sugars constitute less than 10% of total daily energy intake. For an average, moderately active adult who needs about 2000 calories a day, this means less than 50 grams of sugar. Specifically, for women, it can be up to 50 grams (10-12 teaspoons), and for men, up to 60 grams (12-14 teaspoons). However, many of us exceed these recommendations, sometimes by the first half of the day.

In turn, the European Food Safety Authority (EFSA) was unable to establish an upper tolerable intake level for sugar. From EFSA's opinion, it can only be inferred that sugar intake **should be minimized**.

Sugar in Children's Diets

The issue of sugar becomes even more significant when we focus on children's diets. Young bodies are particularly susceptible to the negative effects of excessive sugar consumption, which can manifest not only in weight problems but also in difficulties with concentration and, later in life, in serious health issues. Ensuring proper gut function is crucial in the early years. It is important to provide the right gut bacteria to develop lifelong immunity. However, in today's world, excessive sugar consumption from a young age depletes gut flora, leading to more frequent infections and allergies in children. For example:

- **Children's Breakfast Cereals:**
  They may seem like a healthy choice, but they often contain up to 10-12 grams of sugar per serving, which is almost the equivalent of three teaspoons of sugar.

- **Ice Cream:**
  A favorite treat for many children, a single scoop can contain around 20-25 grams of sugar, which translates to about five teaspoons.

Even products considered "child-friendly," such as fruit juices and granola bars, are often high in added sugar, causing children to unknowingly consume much more sugar than healthy nutrition standards recommend.

The recommended daily intake of sugar for children aged 2 to 18 is no more than 25 grams, which is equivalent to about five to six teaspoons of sugar. In practice, however, many children exceed this limit with just one sugary drink or snack. Therefore, it is crucial for parents and caregivers to be aware of the sugar content in the products they serve to children and to model a healthy approach to nutrition.

Conscious Choices for Children's Health

Managing sugar intake in children begins with the education and examples set by parents and caregivers. By choosing natural snacks like fresh fruits, vegetables with hummus dip, or nuts, we can satisfy children's cravings for sweet flavors while providing them with valuable nutrients. Additionally, preparing homemade versions of sweet dishes, such as cakes or desserts, allows us to control the amount of added sugar, thereby reducing its consumption.

Hidden Sources of Sugar

We often don't realize the amount of sugar we consume because it is hidden in many products that are not traditionally perceived as sweet. Sauces, salad dressings, bread, and even processed meat products can contain significant amounts of added sugar. Therefore, the ability to read labels and recognize different names for sugar, such as high fructose corn syrup, sucrose, or maltose, becomes crucial.

Strategies to Reduce Sugar in Your Diet

Reducing sugar intake doesn't have to mean giving up all things sweet. There are many natural sugar substitutes, such as stevia or erythritol, that can satisfy our sweet cravings without the negative health effects.

Additionally, increasing the consumption of naturally sweet foods like fruits can help reduce the need to reach for sugar.

Practical Changes and Challenges

Changing dietary habits takes time and awareness. You can start with simple steps, such as eliminating sweetened beverages, which are one of the main sources of sugar in many people's diets. Another step is preparing meals at home, which gives you full control over the ingredients and helps avoid hidden sugars.

How to Deal with Hidden Sugar

Ultimately, while sugar provides us with short-term pleasure, the long-term health consequences can be significant. The key to managing sugar intake is awareness. Limit sugar to a minimum, enjoying it occasionally as a treat rather than consuming it daily. Reading labels can reveal how much sugar we're actually consuming. It's also beneficial to look for alternatives to sweetened products—for example, choosing whole-grain bread without added sugars or natural yogurts and adding fresh fruits yourself.

Sugar Addiction

Research shows that sugar can stimulate the same reward pathways in the brain as certain drugs, which can lead to addictive behaviors. This chemical reaction makes the body and mind crave more sugar, leading to a cycle of excessive sugar consumption and increasing the risk of developing negative health effects.

Chronic Inflammation

High sugar intake is also associated with chronic inflammation in the body, which is a risk factor for many chronic diseases, including heart disease and cancer. Inflammation can be triggered by glycation, a process in which excess glucose in the body binds with proteins, forming advanced glycation end-products (AGEs) that can damage tissues.

- ***Increase in Insulin Levels***
  When blood glucose levels rise, the pancreas responds by secreting insulin, a hormone that helps cells absorb glucose from the blood and convert it into energy. Insulin plays a key role in regulating blood sugar levels, but excessive production over a long period can lead to insulin resistance—a condition in which cells become less responsive to the effects of insulin.

- ***Insulin Resistance and Chronic Diseases***
  Chronic excessive sugar consumption can lead to insulin resistance, a condition associated with numerous health problems, including obesity, type 2 diabetes, and even cardiovascular diseases. Insulin resistance hinders effective glucose management, leading to its excessive accumulation in the body and resulting in the aforementioned diseases.

- ***Impact on the Digestive System and Microbiome***
  Sugars, especially refined ones, can also affect the health of the digestive system. They alter the composition of the gut microbiome, which can disrupt the proper bacterial balance and lead to digestive issues such as excessive gas, bloating, and even inflammatory bowel conditions. This state results in chronic

fatigue, reduced immune system function, and a tendency to frequent infections, both viral and allergic.

Scientific Research on Sugar: Impact on Health

Let's now focus on scientific research regarding the impact of sugar on the body's health, highlighting both its key biological roles and the potential health risks associated with its excessive consumption. Controlling sugar intake and consciously managing diet are key steps toward maintaining health and preventing chronic diseases. Here is an overview of key scientific studies on the relationship between sugar consumption and chronic diseases:

Sugar and Cancer – Nobel Prize

Otto Warburg, a Nobel Prize laureate, discovered that cancer cells metabolize glucose differently than healthy cells. This process, known as the Warburg effect, shows that cancer cells prefer glucose fermentation even in the presence of oxygen, which is unusual for most healthy cells that rely on aerobic cellular respiration. This type of metabolism allows cancer cells to quickly generate energy, promoting their rapid growth and spread.

Warburg's discovery has been significant for the development of modern oncology. By understanding that cancer cells are so 'greedy' for sugar, scientists are trying to develop therapies that intentionally disrupt this metabolic process to fight cancer at its core mechanisms. Limiting cancer cells' access to sugar could be key to inhibiting their growth and spread. This fascinating discovery not only opened new doors in the fight against cancer but also emphasizes the importance of understanding the effects of our daily dietary choices.

It's alarming that in today's world, there is insufficient education about proper nutrition and a lack of public awareness about the harm of consuming excessive amounts of sugar in daily diets.

Study on the Impact of Sugar on Inflammation and Cancer Progression

Excessive sugar consumption, especially fructose, can lead to chronic inflammation, which in turn promotes the development and progression of cancer. Studies show that fructose can be a risk factor for various health problems, including hypertension and cardiovascular diseases. Strategies such as lowering uric acid levels, adopting low-fructose diets, and targeting specific enzymes can mitigate these risks.

Sugar and Childhood Obesity

According to a report by Yale scientists, the factors causing childhood obesity differ significantly between richer and poorer countries. In poorer countries, we observe a rise in childhood obesity along with malnutrition. In the USA, the problem is inertia, but awareness of the dangers of sugar and soda consumption is growing. In China, India, and South America, these products are heavily promoted, and soda consumption is very high.

These articles provide comprehensive information on the impact of sugar on chronic diseases, highlighting the importance of diet management and policy interventions to reduce health risks associated with high sugar consumption.

Short Summary - My Daily Life

In my daily life, I avoid sugar, allowing myself to indulge only on special occasions. I believe balance is key, which is why I follow the 80/20 rule.

Eighty percent of my diet consists of healthy, nutritious foods, while the remaining twenty percent includes treats that make life more enjoyable. By adhering to this principle, I may allow myself something sweet, but I usually don't crave it. Occasionally, without guilt, I enjoy a small sweet treat. This approach helps me maintain good health without giving up the small pleasures of daily life. I believe our bodies are strong enough to handle occasional indulgences if we take proper care of them daily.

In home, I use erythritol, sometimes xylitol, and honey. These products add sweetness to baked goods and are healthier alternatives to sugar. They work well in baking cakes, pancakes, and desserts, allowing enjoyment of sweet flavors without the negative health impact. Erythritol and stevia are natural sweeteners that do not raise blood sugar levels, while xylitol, though caloric, has a lower glycemic index than sugar. Honey, besides sweetness, provides valuable nutrients and has antibacterial properties. In my kitchen, these natural sweeteners have become essential ingredients in healthy and delicious recipes.

Here is an example:

Recipe: Blueberry Muffins

Ingredients:

- 1 cup almond flour
- ¼ cup plant-based milk (almond or coconut)
- 1 large egg
- 2 tablespoons erythritol
- 2 teaspoons baking powder
- A pinch of salt
- 125 g blueberries
- Oil for greasing the muffin tins

Preparation:

1. Mix the almond flour with baking powder, salt, and erythritol. Add the egg and milk. Mix everything thoroughly.
2. Fill the muffin tins to 1/4 of their height with the batter. Gently press a few blueberries into the batter and add another portion of batter. Place the remaining blueberries on top.
3. Put the tins in an oven preheated to 180°C and bake for about 15 minutes.
4. Remove and let cool.

You can find more "sweet" recipes, along with a shopping list, in my book: ***"Sugar, Gluten, and Dairy-Free Recipes"***

Summary, examining the impact of excessive sugar consumption on our health, it becomes clear how important it is to make conscious dietary choices to minimize the risk of lifestyle diseases. Excess sugar in the diet contributes to obesity, type 2 diabetes, skin problems, and many other ailments. However, sugar is not the only ingredient whose excess in the diet can lead to serious health issues.

Another important topic worth discussing is trans fats—hidden enemies in our food that, like excess sugar, can have disastrous effects on health. In the upcoming chapter, we will look at what trans fats are, which products contain the most of them, and the health consequences of their consumption. We will also discover how to avoid these dangerous fats and what to replace them with in our daily diet to maintain health and well-being.

CHAPTER 3

Trans Fats - Unassuming Enemies

We live in a modern world full of processed foods and quick meals. In the daily rush, it's easy to forget about the ingredients we consume every day. However, unconscious dietary choices can lead to serious health consequences, especially when it comes to trans fats and saturated fats. These two types of fats, though different in chemical structure and source, have one thing in common—they can both be unassuming enemies of our health.

Trans Fats - The Silent Killer

Trans fats are a particular type of unsaturated fat created through a process called hydrogenation. This process involves adding hydrogen atoms to vegetable oil molecules, altering their chemical structure. Hydrogenation is often used by the food industry because the resulting hardened oils are more stable, have a longer shelf life, and provide better texture, which is attractive to food manufacturers, especially in the production of baked goods, snacks, fried foods, and margarines.

Health Effects

Trans fats are particularly dangerous for our cardiovascular health. They increase levels of "bad" LDL cholesterol in the blood, which can lead to the formation of atherosclerotic plaques on artery walls. These plaques narrow the arteries, increasing the risk of heart attack and stroke. Moreover, trans fats lower levels of "good" HDL cholesterol, which helps remove cholesterol from the bloodstream, protecting against heart disease.

Research indicates that regular consumption of trans fats may also contribute to the development of type 2 diabetes. This mechanism is related to the impact of trans fats on insulin resistance—a condition in which the body's cells become less sensitive to insulin. This leads to higher blood glucose levels, which is characteristic of diabetes.

Trans fats can also affect inflammation in the body. Studies show that they can increase levels of inflammatory markers, such as C-reactive protein (CRP), which are associated with a higher risk of many chronic diseases, including heart disease, diabetes, and other inflammation-related health conditions.

Long-term consumption of trans fats can also lead to an increased risk of certain types of cancer. The negative health effects associated with trans fats are extensively documented, and avoiding these fats in the diet is a step towards improving overall health and increasing lifespan.

Identifying and Avoiding Trans Fats

Although some sectors of the food industry have started to limit the use of trans fats due to their negative health effects, they can still be found in many products. Manufacturers often reduce the amount of trans fats in their products but do not eliminate them entirely, which means we are exposed to them daily, especially when consuming processed foods, quick snacks, or sweets. Therefore, it is crucial to skillfully read food labels, which may hide trans fats under names such as "partially hydrogenated vegetable oils." Sometimes these fats may also be listed as "hardened fats" or "hydrogenated fats."

Avoiding products containing these ingredients is the best way to reduce the risk of serious health problems such as heart disease or diabetes. Regularly checking labels and choosing products that clearly state they contain no trans fats can significantly improve the quality of your diet and overall health.

Where Trans Fats Hide

Trans fats can be found in many processed food products, where they are mainly used for their technological properties, such as extending shelf life, improving texture, and adding flavor. Here are examples of products that may contain trans fats:

- **Margarines and Fat Spreads:**
  Solid margarine, in particular, can contain trans fats resulting from the hydrogenation process.

- **Butter:**
  While butter contains high amounts of vitamins A, β-carotene, and smaller amounts of vitamins D and E, it also contains trans fatty acids.

- **Processed Cheese and Spreads:**
  Especially processed, homogenized, or spreadable cheeses. Spreading butter on bread and then adding processed cheese can be extremely harmful to health. Avoiding these eating habits is advisable.

- **Instant Soups and Sauces:**
  Popular instant soups and powdered sauces, including so-called "Chinese" noodles, also contain trans isomers.

- **Fast Food:**
  Products like fries, hamburgers, and nuggets can contain trans fats, especially if fried in partially hydrogenated oils.

- **Cookies, Cakes, and Pastries:**
  Many commercially produced sweets and baked goods contain trans fats to achieve the desired texture and shelf life.

- **Snack Foods like Chips:**
  Chips and other fried snacks may contain trans fats, used for their stability at high temperatures during production.

- **Frozen Ready Meals:**
  Pizzas, casseroles, and other frozen ready meals may contain trans fats in ingredients such as dough or sauces.

- **Coffee Creamers and Some Plant-Based Milks:**
  These products may contain trans fats added to improve consistency and flavor.

- **Artificial Creams:**
  Often contain trans fats that help maintain the product's stability and creamy texture.

A healthy diet requires careful reading of food labels to avoid trans fats. Looking for words like "partially hydrogenated oils" can help identify products containing undesirable fats. Eliminating or significantly reducing the consumption of products containing trans fats is an important step towards maintaining a healthy lifestyle.

Alternatives and Dietary Choices

Healthy alternatives to trans fats include unsaturated fats, such as plant oils (olive oil, flaxseed oil), which are beneficial for heart health. It's also important to incorporate monounsaturated and polyunsaturated fats into your diet, which can be found in avocados, nuts, and fish. Properly balancing the types of fats in your diet can significantly improve your lipid profile and overall health.

Although saturated fats are often viewed negatively, the key to benefiting from them is moderation and awareness of their sources. They naturally occur in many products that offer valuable nutrients. For example, red meat provides not only saturated fats but also vitamins like A and D, as well as important minerals. Additionally, products like butter and lard are traditional sources of saturated fats in many cultures. Unlike solid margarine, lard may not contain trans fats. It's important to consider the origin of products, as those available in stores might contain harmful trans fats.

Key to Health: Balance

An essential aspect of a healthy diet is balance and the ability to combine saturated fats with other types of fats that have beneficial effects on health, such as monounsaturated and polyunsaturated fats. Incorporating plant-based fats, such as olive oil or flaxseed oil, can help achieve this balance. Instead of completely eliminating saturated fats, it's better to limit them to recommended levels, which depend on age, gender, and individual health needs. The World Health Organization recommends limiting trans fat intake to less than 1% of total daily caloric intake, which translates to about 2 grams per day on a 2000-calorie diet.

How to Use Fats Wisely

- ⇨ **Choose Products from Good Sources:**
  Prefer organic products and fats from grass-fed animals raised in good conditions, which can increase the content of beneficial components like omega-3 fatty acids.

- ⇨ **Cook at Low Temperatures:**
  Saturated fats are more stable when cooking at high temperatures compared to some unsaturated fats, making them a better choice for frying. However, always remember to avoid burning fats, as this can lead to the formation of harmful chemical compounds.

- ⇨ **Combine with Vegetables:**
  Consuming saturated fats as part of a balanced meal that also contains plenty of vegetables can increase the health benefits of the meal by improving the absorption of fat-soluble vitamins found in vegetables.

Awareness is the First Step

A key element in preventing the negative health effects associated with trans and saturated fats is being aware of what is in our diet. These fats are often hidden in processed foods, fast food, and even some "healthy" snacks that can be misleadingly marketed as good for health. Therefore, it is crucial to learn how to recognize and avoid products that contain them.

Identifying Fats on Labels

The first step is learning to read product labels. Food manufacturers are required to list ingredients on packaging, which means we can check if a product contains harmful fats. Pay special attention to phrases such as "partially hydrogenated oils" or "palm oil"—these can indicate the presence of trans fats. Learning to identify these ingredients may take some time, but it is an investment in long-term health.

Which Fats Are Best for Frying?

Let's start with a fundamental question: which fat is best for frying? Each fat has unique properties determined by its chemical structure. This structure decides whether a fat is suitable for frying.

Fats are made up of fatty acids, which can be compared to the bricks that build a house. There are three main types of fatty acids:

- ✓ **Saturated Fatty Acids:**
  They have only single chemical bonds between carbon atoms. They are very stable and resistant to high temperatures. Examples: butter, lard, coconut oil, palm oil.

- ✓ **Monounsaturated Fatty Acids:**
  They have one double bond between carbon atoms, making them less stable than saturated fatty acids. Examples: olive oil, canola oil, avocado oil.

- ✓ **Polyunsaturated Fatty Acids:**
  They contain multiple double bonds, making them the most unstable and prone to oxidation at high temperatures. Examples: flaxseed oil, sunflower oil, soybean oil, pumpkin seed oil, fish oils.

Many of you probably know that flaxseed oil is particularly prone to oxidation and quick spoilage. Therefore, it is recommended to purchase it only when it is freshly pressed. Even at normal temperatures, such as room temperature or refrigerator storage, this oil quickly loses its properties.

Now imagine what happens to this oil when it is subjected to high temperatures. Warmer temperatures will cause the fatty acids in flaxseed oil to oxidize quickly. The product will lose its most important properties, and consuming it will become pointless. This happens because flaxseed oil is mainly composed of polyunsaturated fatty acids.

For this reason, frying is not recommended with oils high in polyunsaturated fatty acids. Examples of such oils were mentioned earlier, but it is worth reiterating that one of them is the popular sunflower oil. Unfortunately, using it for frying is one of the biggest dietary mistakes we can make.

Remember that oils rich in polyunsaturated fatty acids should be used exclusively unrefined and served cold, e.g., as an addition to salads or sandwich spreads.

Which Fats to Choose?

Therefore, it is worth choosing fats that are as minimally processed as possible. Saturated and monounsaturated fats are best for frying because they are more stable at high temperatures. Here are some recommendations:

- ✓ **Ghee (Clarified Butter):**
  Ideal for frying due to its high smoke point and lack of proteins that could burn.

- ✓ **Coconut Oil:**
  Stable at high temperatures, rich in saturated fatty acids, which are less prone to oxidation.

- ✓ **Olive Oil:**
  Especially extra virgin, is rich in monounsaturated fatty acids and has moderate thermal stability.

- ✓ **Avocado Oil:**
  Has a high smoke point and is rich in monounsaturated fats.

- ✓ **Lard:**
  If for some reason you decide on long-term frying, which is not encouraged, you could also consider lard or coconut oil. Even better options would be goose fat or duck fat. These last two options are considered some of the best for frying.

Avoid frying with oils that are high in polyunsaturated fatty acids, such as sunflower, soybean, or flaxseed oil, as they are more prone to oxidation at high temperatures.

Practical Tips

- ⇨ **Read product labels** and avoid ingredients like "partially hydrogenated vegetable oils."
- ⇨ **Choose products** containing healthy unsaturated fats, such as olive oil, hemp oil, or flaxseed oil.
- ⇨ **Avoid fast foods** and processed snacks, which often contain trans fats.
- ⇨ **Incorporate more fatty fish, nuts, and avocados** into your diet, as they are rich in healthy fats.

By making conscious dietary choices, you can significantly improve your health and reduce the risk of serious diseases. Being aware of what is in your diet is key to maintaining good health. Making informed dietary decisions, avoiding processed foods, and replacing harmful fats with healthier alternatives are essential steps towards better health and a longer life.

According to WHO Studies

Cardiovascular diseases are the leading cause of death worldwide. The main risk factors include unhealthy diet, lack of physical activity, tobacco use, and alcohol consumption. Among dietary factors, high trans fat intake increases the risk of death from any cause by 34%, deaths from coronary heart disease by 28%, and coronary heart disease by 21%. Trans fats have no known health benefits.

Trans fat is industrially produced by partially hydrogenating any liquid oils, mostly vegetable oils, but it also occurs naturally in meat and dairy products from ruminants. In a healthy diet, the recommended intake of trans fats is less than 1% of total energy. Industrially produced trans fats are not part of a healthy diet and should be avoided.

Governments play a crucial role in creating a healthy food environment that enables people to adopt and maintain healthy dietary practices. They must encourage the reformulation of food products to reduce trans fat content and eliminate industrially produced trans fats.

Short Summary - My Daily Life

Let's go back to thinking about our home and car. Trans fats can be compared to old, burnt oil in a car. Just as contaminated oil makes the engine run less efficiently, trans fats negatively impact our health.

Healthy fats, such as those from avocados, nuts, olive oil, and fish, nourish the body and support its proper functioning. They can be compared to new oil, which, after being changed, makes the car's engine run better and more efficiently. Incorporating healthy unsaturated fats into the diet can significantly improve our lipid profile and overall health, just as fresh oil improves a car's performance.

In home, I use a range of different fats, both plant-based and animal-based. I use plant-based fats mainly cold, for salads, dips, or pesto. In my kitchen, you can find plant oils such as olive oil, hemp oil, avocado oil, MCT oil, grape seed oil, pumpkin seed oil, sesame oil, and coconut oil.

Due to their resistance to high temperatures and high smoke points, I also use animal fats. They are ideal for frying (which I do rarely or very quickly), using goose, duck, or beef lard, or ghee—clarified butter free of casein, the cow's milk protein. This can be used without issue by those with dairy intolerance. Ghee is perfect for morning scrambled eggs or vegetables.

Remember that it is worth consciously choosing the products we consume, paying attention to the quality of fats we provide to our bodies. By eliminating trans fats from the diet and replacing them with healthier options, we can improve our health and well-being.

Fun Fact: Salt and Heat Processing of Fats

Did you know that the presence of salt during the heat processing of fats can accelerate their oxidation? Salt, long a controversial topic in nutrition, affects many processes occurring in food, including fat oxidation. Studies clearly show that salt can facilitate this process, which can impact the quality and nutritional value of dishes.

What Can Be Done?

To reduce the risk of fat oxidation during frying, avoid adding salt before or during frying. It is best to salt dishes only at the end of cooking. The same rules can be applied to braising—add salt at the very end to preserve as many nutrients as possible and avoid unfavorable chemical reactions.

After understanding the impact of trans and saturated fats on our health, it's important to look at another common ingredient in our diet—gluten. In the next chapter, we will discuss what gluten is, its properties, and how it affects our health, particularly in the context of people with celiac disease and gluten intolerance. We will also explore how to avoid gluten and what alternatives can be incorporated into the diet.

CHAPTER 4

Gluten - Necessary Nuisance?

Gluten is a protein found in many grains such as wheat, barley, and rye. It is known for its ability to give elasticity and structure to baked goods, making it indispensable in the production of bread, pasta, and many other food products. It plays a key role in kitchens worldwide. However, in recent years, gluten has become a hot topic of debate and interest among consumers and scientists alike.

We will now look at various aspects of gluten, examining its impact on health, why some people need to avoid it, and what alternatives exist for those who are gluten intolerant or wish to reduce its consumption in their diet. We will also consider the trend of gluten-free diets and their real impact on health.

The Impact of Gluten on Health

For most people, gluten is considered completely safe and does not cause any negative health effects. But is that really the case? For some individuals, consuming gluten leads to health problems, the most well-known being celiac disease—an autoimmune disorder that can damage the small intestine in genetically predisposed individuals. Other less severe reactions include gluten intolerance and wheat allergy, which can also cause discomfort and health issues.

In today's world, more and more people are feeling fatigued, experiencing skin problems, digestive issues, recurrent swelling, and are unsure why. Could gluten be the culprit?

Gluten in the Modern Diet: Why Is It a Problem?

Contemporary changes in grain production and food processing have influenced our perception and bodily reaction to gluten. Although gluten has been part of the human diet for thousands of years, modern methods of cultivation, grain breeding, and food processing have made it problematic for many people.

Intensification of Cultivation and Changes in Grain Genetics

- ***Changes in Grain Genetics:***
  Modern plant breeding methods have focused on increasing the yield and disease resistance of grains, often involving the modification of their genetic composition. These changes may have affected the structure of proteins, including gluten, making it more difficult to digest for some people.

- ***Intensive Cultivation:***
  To meet the growing demand for food, agriculture intensively uses pesticides and fertilizers, which can impact the chemical composition of plants, including gluten content. Residues of these substances in products can further burden the digestive system.

Food Processing and Diet

- ***Processed Products:***
  The rise in consumption of processed foods, which are often rich in gluten, exposes us to an excess of gluten in our diets. Many processed products contain gluten as an additive to improve texture and taste, increasing its presence in everyday meals.

- ***Changes in Diet:***
  Modern diets are often characterized by less diversity and a higher proportion of processed grain products. This makes gluten present in most meals, potentially contributing to the development of intolerance and sensitivity to this ingredient.

Where is Gluten Found?

Gluten naturally occurs in several types of grains. Here are the grains that contain gluten:

- **Wheat:**
  Products made from wheat contain gluten, such as bread, pasta, bulgur, semolina, couscous, cakes, cookies, breakfast cereals, and baked goods containing wheat flour.

- **Barley:**
  Barley contains gluten, so avoid products such as pearl barley, barley malt, barley beer, and certain syrups and extracts used as sweeteners or flavorings.

- **Rye:**
  Rye also contains gluten. Avoid products like rye bread, certain types of flour, sausages containing rye, and certain alcoholic beverages like rye vodka.

- **Oats:**
  Naturally, oats do not contain gluten, but they are often contaminated with gluten during processing. Look for "gluten-free" labels on oat products.

Additionally, gluten may also be present in other food products as an additive or ingredient, such as:

- **Sauces and Soups:**
  Some sauces and soups may contain gluten in the form of thickeners or stabilizers, e.g., soy sauce, teriyaki sauce, bouillon cubes, powdered soups, etc. Choose gluten-free versions.

- **Confectionery and Sweets:**
  Cakes, cookies, cupcakes, desserts, and many other sweets usually contain gluten because they use wheat flour.

How Gluten Affects Our Health

While gluten is an integral part of the diet for many, it can be a source of serious health problems for others, particularly those with celiac disease or gluten intolerance and sensitivity. Here is how gluten can affect our health in the long term.

Chronic Inflammation

For people intolerant to gluten, its consumption leads to an autoimmune reaction that attacks the small intestine, causing inflammation. This chronic inflammation not only damages the intestinal lining but can also contribute to a wide range of health problems. Chronic inflammation is considered a risk factor for many chronic diseases, including:

- ***Cardiovascular Diseases:***
  Chronic inflammation can lead to atherosclerosis, the hardening and narrowing of the arteries, increasing the risk of heart attack and stroke.

- ***Type 2 Diabetes:***
  Inflammation can affect how the body uses insulin, contributing to insulin resistance, and ultimately leading to type 2 diabetes.

- ***Autoimmune Diseases:***
  Chronic inflammation associated with gluten intolerance can trigger or exacerbate other autoimmune diseases such as rheumatoid arthritis, systemic lupus erythematosus, or Hashimoto's thyroiditis.

- ***Neurological Diseases:***
  Inflammation can impact the nervous system, leading to neurological symptoms such as migraines, neuropathy, and even neurodegenerative diseases, including multiple sclerosis.

- ***Digestive Problems:***
  Chronic intestinal inflammation can cause other digestive issues like irritable bowel syndrome (IBS) and other inflammatory bowel diseases such as Crohn's disease or ulcerative colitis.

- ***Osteoporosis:***
  Chronic inflammation can affect the body's ability to absorb essential nutrients, potentially leading to osteoporosis, which increases the risk of fractures and other bone-related problems.

- ***Mental Health:***
  Inflammation can also impact mental health, contributing to depression, anxiety, and other mood disorders. Studies indicate that individuals with gluten intolerance may be more susceptible to these health issues.

Understanding the wide range of diseases that can be associated with chronic inflammation caused by gluten intolerance is crucial for managing health and avoiding potential complications. We must recognize that food can be both medicine and poison.

Health Awareness and Diagnostics

- **Improved Diagnostics:**
  Increased awareness of celiac disease and gluten intolerance has led to more people being diagnosed with these conditions. This, in turn, affects the perception of gluten as a harmful factor.

- **Understanding Health Impact:**
  Understanding the link between diet and health has helped identify gluten as a potential culprit for health problems such as inflammation, digestive issues, and autoimmune diseases.

How to Minimize Negative Effects

Individuals diagnosed with celiac disease or gluten intolerance can significantly improve their health and quality of life by completely eliminating gluten from their diet. Making a conscious decision to eliminate gluten, as well as understanding and managing inflammation, can greatly help reduce the risk of long-term health problems.

So, what are the main health issues associated with gluten? Let's take a closer look at the most important ones, starting with celiac disease.

Celiac Disease

Celiac disease can significantly impact the daily lives of those affected. It is rooted in an intolerance to gluten, a protein found in wheat, barley, and rye. In individuals with celiac disease, consuming gluten triggers an autoimmune response in which the immune system attacks the body's own tissues—in this case, the villi of the small intestine.

Mechanism of the Disease

The villi are tiny finger-like projections lining the small intestine, responsible for nutrient absorption. Damage to these structures due to the immune response leads to their atrophy, resulting in poor absorption of essential nutrients. Individuals with celiac disease can experience chronic deficiencies in substances such as iron, vitamins, as well as proteins and carbohydrates, further affecting overall health.

Symptoms and Effects

Celiac disease can manifest in various ways, ranging from mild to very severe. Typical symptoms include abdominal pain, diarrhea, bloating, as well as chronic fatigue and anemia. Some individuals may also experience non-gastrointestinal symptoms, such as skin rashes, joint pain, and even neurological problems.

Long-Term Consequences

Prolonged exposure to gluten in untreated individuals with celiac disease can lead to more severe health problems, such as osteoporosis, which is the weakening of bones due to calcium deficiency, and an increased risk of developing certain types of cancers, including celiac-associated lymphoma and small bowel cancer. Additionally, celiac disease can affect fertility in both women and men.

Diagnosis and Treatment

Diagnosing celiac disease typically requires a series of tests, including blood tests for antibodies and a biopsy of the small intestine to confirm villi damage. Although there is currently no cure for celiac disease, effective management involves strictly adhering to a gluten-free diet, which allows the villi to heal and alleviates symptoms.

Living with Celiac Disease

Adopting a gluten-free diet can be challenging, but with proper support and education, individuals with celiac disease can lead healthy and active lives. It is essential to avoid products containing gluten, including many types of bread, pasta, and numerous processed food products that may contain hidden gluten.

In summary, celiac disease is a serious condition that requires a strict gluten-free diet. But what about individuals who experience symptoms but do not have celiac disease? Let's now consider the issue of gluten intolerance.

Non-Celiac Gluten Sensitivity

While celiac disease is a serious autoimmune disorder, many people experience symptoms of gluten intolerance without a celiac diagnosis. This intolerance, known as non-celiac gluten sensitivity (NCGS), can also cause significant discomfort. Let's take a closer look at this condition.

NCGS poses diagnostic and therapeutic challenges for many individuals who do not meet the criteria for celiac disease but still react negatively to gluten consumption. This form of intolerance does not involve the autoimmune damage to the intestines characteristic of celiac disease but can cause a range of unpleasant and uncomfortable symptoms.

Symptoms and Diagnosis

Symptoms of NCGS can vary widely and include both digestive and extra-intestinal issues. Common complaints include abdominal pain, bloating, diarrhea or constipation, swelling, weight gain or loss, as well as general fatigue, headaches, brain fog, and even depression. These symptoms are often nonspecific, making it difficult to attribute them directly to gluten intolerance.

Diagnosis of NCGS is typically based on the exclusion of other potential causes of symptoms, including celiac disease and wheat allergy. This process usually involves maintaining a detailed food diary, which can help identify the relationship between gluten consumption and the occurrence of symptoms. Modern diagnostic methods such as bioresonance testing can also be used to determine the body's sensitivity to foods that cause harm. An elimination diet free of gluten, followed by a deliberate and gradual reintroduction of gluten, can also serve as a diagnostic tool.

Management and Treatment

The primary and most effective treatment for NCGS is the elimination of gluten from the diet. Although this can be challenging, many individuals experience significant improvements in their health and quality of life once they stop consuming gluten-containing products.

The growing gluten-free food market offers more options, making it easier to find suitable products in most supermarkets. While dietary changes can be difficult, the wide range of gluten-free products available today helps make the transition easier.

Education and Support

Education about gluten intolerance and available dietary options is crucial for individuals dealing with this condition. Many health organizations and support groups offer resources and support to help those with gluten intolerance lead full and healthy gluten-free lives. Regular consultations with a dietitian specializing in elimination diets can also provide necessary guidance and support in managing the diet.

Everyone reacts to gluten differently, so it is important that the dietary approach is tailored to individual needs and the body's specific reactions.

In summary, NCGS is a condition in which individuals experience symptoms similar to celiac disease, even though tests for celiac disease are negative. Despite the lack of a full understanding of the mechanism of this condition, eliminating gluten from the diet brings relief from symptoms.

But what about people who have a wheat allergy? How does this condition differ from gluten intolerance, and what are its specific characteristics?

Let's now delve into the detailed discussion of wheat allergy to understand its mechanisms, symptoms, and diagnostic methods.

Wheat Allergy

Gluten intolerance is not the only reaction some people may have to wheat consumption. Another significant condition is wheat allergy, which can manifest in various ways and requires a specific approach to diagnosis and treatment.

Wheat allergy is one of the better-known allergic reactions associated with the consumption of plant proteins, particularly those present in wheat. It is a condition that can affect many aspects of daily life, from food choices to social interactions and the emotional impact of dietary restrictions.

Symptoms of Wheat Allergy

Individuals with a wheat allergy can experience a range of symptoms depending on the severity of their sensitivity. The most common reactions include abdominal pain, nausea, vomiting, diarrhea, and skin reactions such as rashes, hives, itching, and even eczema. Respiratory symptoms are also common, including sneezing, coughing, difficulty breathing, and asthma. In the most severe cases, wheat allergy can lead to anaphylaxis, a condition requiring immediate medical intervention due to the risk of life-threatening allergic shock.

Diagnosis and Management of Wheat Allergy

Diagnosing wheat allergy often involves a detailed medical history and allergy tests, such as skin prick tests or blood tests. It is essential to differentiate wheat allergy from celiac disease and gluten intolerance, as they have different underlying mechanisms and require different therapeutic approaches.

Managing wheat allergy primarily involves the complete avoidance of wheat and wheat-containing products. This requires thorough knowledge of food ingredients and the ability to read product labels. Additionally, it is advisable always to carry antihistamines or, in cases at risk of anaphylaxis, an epinephrine auto-injector.

For individuals who must avoid wheat and gluten, dietary changes can lead to significant health improvements. But what is life like without gluten? Let's explore naturally gluten-free products and alternatives to traditional gluten-containing foods.

Living Without Gluten

Following a gluten-free diet, while it may seem challenging, is becoming increasingly manageable due to the growing availability of gluten-free products and a better understanding of how to live without gluten. Proper education and knowledge of naturally gluten-free foods are crucial for enjoying a healthy and fulfilling life without the risk of negative health effects.

Naturally Gluten-Free Products

Many staple foods are naturally gluten-free. Here is a list of gluten-free products (if not contaminated with gluten):

- ✓ **Rice:**
  One of the most popular substitutes for gluten-containing grains, available in many varieties, from white to brown.

- ✓ **Grains:**
  Such as buckwheat, quinoa, amaranth, sorghum, and millet, which are excellent sources of protein and fiber.

- ✓ **Vegetables and Fruits:**
  Naturally gluten-free and can be eaten in any form. This includes corn, soy, tapioca, and potatoes (including potato flour).

- ✓ **Meat and Fish:**
  Poultry, beef, pork, fish, and seafood are gluten-free sources of protein.

- ✓ **Milk and Dairy Products:**
  Natural milk, yogurt, butter, cottage cheese, and cheese are gluten-free. However, ensure that dairy products do not contain additives or ingredients that may contain gluten.

- ✓ **Eggs:**
  Naturally gluten-free.

- ✓ **Legumes:**
  Beans, lentils, chickpeas, peas, sesame seeds, flaxseeds, sunflower seeds, pumpkin seeds, and other legumes and seeds are naturally gluten-free.

- ✓ **Nuts and Fats:**
  Naturally gluten-free. However, ensure that nuts do not contain additives or ingredients that may contain gluten.

By incorporating these naturally gluten-free foods into your diet, you can maintain a balanced and nutritious diet while avoiding gluten. This approach will help manage conditions like celiac disease, non-celiac gluten sensitivity, and wheat allergy, ensuring a healthy lifestyle.

Alternatives to Gluten-Containing Products

Thanks to advances in the food industry, there are numerous alternatives to traditional gluten-containing products available on the market, making it easier to follow a gluten-free diet. These include:

- ✓ **Gluten-Free Flours:**
  Such as rice flour, coconut flour, chickpea flour, which can replace traditional wheat flour in baking and cooking.
- ✓ **Gluten-Free Pasta and Bread:**
  An increasing number of brands offer high-quality pasta, bread, and other bakery products that do not contain gluten.
- ✓ **Ready Meals and Snacks:**
  From gluten-free pizzas to bars and cookies, there are many options available for those on a gluten-free diet.

With these alternatives, maintaining a gluten-free diet becomes more convenient and varied, allowing for a satisfying and balanced dietary experience.

Considerations for Gluten-Free Products

While gluten-free alternatives are readily available, it is important to pay attention to their ingredients. These products can often contain more sugar, fats, or chemical additives to improve taste and texture, which can have undesirable health effects:

- ***High Calorie Content:***
  Some gluten-free products may have higher calorie content than their gluten-containing counterparts.

- ***Additives and Preservatives:***
  To achieve the desired consistency and flavor, manufacturers may add substances to gluten-free products that are not always beneficial for health.

Being mindful of these factors can help ensure that a gluten-free diet remains healthy and balanced.

Lifestyle Changes

Living without gluten also requires certain lifestyle and dietary habit changes:

- ***Reading Labels:***
  Being able to identify gluten-containing ingredients is crucial. Look for products with a "gluten-free" certification and always carefully check labels.

- ***Avoiding Cross-Contamination:***
  In a kitchen where gluten-containing products are also prepared, it's essential to use separate utensils and surfaces for preparing gluten-free meals.

- ***Education and Support:***
  Joining support groups or forums for people with celiac disease can help in exchanging experiences, recipes, and tips on how to effectively live without gluten.

Understanding and adapting your diet and lifestyle to meet gluten-free needs can help avoid negative health effects and enjoy life fully without compromising on taste and meal variety.

Understanding the Gluten-Free Diet: Not Just a Trend, But a Necessity

In recent years, the gluten-free diet has become very popular, often seen as a health option or even a trendy lifestyle choice. However, for many people, avoiding gluten is not a matter of preference but a health necessity.

Impact of Gluten on Individuals with Intolerance and Celiac Disease

For those with celiac disease, gluten intolerance, or wheat allergy, consuming gluten-containing products can lead to severe health problems, ranging from abdominal pain and an increased risk of osteoporosis to life-threatening anaphylaxis. For them, a gluten-free diet is the only way to avoid these reactions and maintain their health.

Social Education and Eliminating Stereotypes

It is important for society to understand that while some individuals choose a gluten-free diet for personal reasons or as a lifestyle element, for others, it is a strict medical requirement. Distinguishing between a trend and a medical necessity will help eliminate stereotypes and increase awareness of celiac disease and other related health conditions.

Availability and Identification of Gluten-Free Products

Improving the availability of gluten-free options in restaurants, stores, and other public facilities is also crucial. Clear labeling of gluten-free products and educating food service workers about safely handling gluten-free foods can significantly ease the lives of those on a gluten-free diet.

Beloved Bread

A gluten-free diet doesn't mean completely giving up on bread. Gluten-free bread is becoming increasingly popular, especially among people with celiac disease, gluten sensitivity, and those who simply want to eliminate gluten from their diet.

Why Bake Gluten-Free Bread at Home?

Baking your own gluten-free bread ensures that you know exactly what's in your food. It gives you control over the ingredients you consume, which is undoubtedly a big advantage for those striving to lead a healthy lifestyle.

Baking gluten-free bread at home is not only a way to maintain a healthy diet but also an opportunity to develop your culinary skills. Remember, experimenting with different ingredients and baking techniques is the best way to discover your favorite gluten-free bread recipe. See for yourself how satisfying it can be to bake your own healthy bread.

What Ingredients Are Needed to Bake Gluten-Free Bread?

Starting your journey with baking gluten-free bread can feel a bit daunting. Will the gluten-free bread taste good? Is it difficult to prepare? Can we find the right ingredients? The answer to these questions is simple—gluten-free bread can be just as tasty, if not more flavorful, than traditional bread. Preparing it is not complicated. And the ingredients? You really only need a few basics:

- ✓ **Gluten-Free Flour:**
  The foundation of any bread, including gluten-free bread, is, of course, flour. Various types of gluten-free flour are available on the market, such as rice flour, corn flour, buckwheat flour, oat

flour, amaranth flour, or quinoa flour. Each has its unique properties that affect the taste and texture of the final product, offering endless possibilities for experimentation.

- ✓ **Gluten-Free Yeast:**
  Yeast is an essential ingredient for bread, responsible for making the dough rise. Fresh yeast and dried yeast usually do not contain gluten. However, remember that not all yeast products are gluten-free, so always check the labels.

- ✓ **Additions and Variations:**
  Depending on whether you want dark, whole grain bread or light and fluffy bread, you can add various grains, nuts, seeds, or even dried fruits to the dough. The choice of additions is vast, allowing you to customize the recipe to your taste preferences.

Gluten-free bread is not only a healthy but also a delicious choice. With these basic ingredients and some patience, you can start your adventure with baking gluten-free bread today. Who knows, you might discover a true baking master within yourself!

Tips and Tricks for Baking Gluten-Free Bread for the First Time

Baking gluten-free bread can seem challenging, especially if you're doing it for the first time. But don't worry, it's a process that can be easily mastered. Here are a few tips and tricks to help you bake the perfect gluten-free bread:

- ⇨ **Choosing Flour:**
  There are many different types of gluten-free flours you can use for baking bread. Rice flour, corn flour, tapioca flour, buckwheat

flour, and oat flour all have different properties and flavors that can affect the final product. Experiment with different flours to find the one that suits you best.

⇨ **Hydration:**
Gluten-free bread often requires more water than traditional bread. Always have extra water on hand while mixing the dough.

⇨ **Rising Time:**
Gluten-free bread dough may need more time to rise. Allow it to double in size before putting it in the oven.

⇨ **Moistening the Bread During Baking:**
To achieve a beautiful, crispy crust, spray the bread with water a few times during baking.

⇨ **Patience:**
Baking gluten-free bread is a process that requires patience. Don't get discouraged if the first few tries aren't perfect. Each attempt will bring you more experience and better results.

Above all, remember that baking bread is not only a way to prepare a healthy and tasty meal but also a lot of fun. Enjoy the process and experiment, and you will soon master the art of baking gluten-free bread.

Recipe: Fluffy Gluten-Free Yeast Bread

Ingredients:

- 3 cups rice flour
- 1 cup potato starch
- 1 teaspoon salt
- 2 teaspoons honey
- 2 teaspoons gluten-free yeast
- 2 tablespoons olive oil
- 2 cups of warm water (enough to make the dough)

Preparation:

1. In a bowl, combine the dry ingredients: rice flour, potato starch, salt, and yeast.
2. Add the olive oil and warm water mixed with honey, then mix everything until you get a uniform consistency.
3. Transfer the dough to a greased bread pan and let it rise for about an hour.
4. Preheat the oven to 180°C (350°F) and bake the bread for about 40-45 minutes, until the bread is golden and crispy.

Enjoy your fluffy gluten-free yeast bread!

A Healthy Gluten-Free Option:

Recipe: Chicken Curry with Broccoli and Green Beans

Ingredients:

- 2 chicken fillets
- 1 red bell pepper
- 1 yellow bell pepper
- 2 cloves of garlic
- 1 can of coconut milk (unsweetened)
- 2 tablespoons curry paste (ensure it's gluten and sugar-free)
- 1 zucchini
- 1 small broccoli
- 200g green beans

- 2 tablespoons coconut oil or olive oil
- 1 teaspoon turmeric
- 1 tablespoon gluten-free soy sauce
- 1 tablespoon gluten-free fish sauce
- 1 chili pepper (optional)
- Fresh cilantro for garnish (optional)

Preparation:

1. Cut the chicken fillets into cubes.
2. In a large pan, heat the coconut oil or olive oil. Add the cubed chicken and lightly sauté.
3. Add garlic, chili, soy sauce, and fish sauce. Mix well.
4. Add the sliced bell peppers, zucchini, broccoli florets, and chopped green beans.
5. Add the curry paste to the vegetables, pour in the coconut milk, and mix thoroughly.
6. Cook on low heat for about 10-15 minutes until the vegetables are tender.
7. Serve hot, garnished with fresh cilantro (if using).
8. You can diversify the dish by serving it with brown rice.

For more recipes for breakfast, lunch, dinner, dessert, and gluten-free bread and rolls, check out my book: ***"Sugar, Gluten, and Dairy-Free Recipes".***

Understanding the impact of gluten on health and exploring its alternatives is a crucial step in maintaining our well-being. Just like gluten, other proteins can also trigger various reactions in our bodies, affecting health and well-being. Spreading knowledge about gluten and related health issues is key to building a more informed society and better support for those who must avoid gluten out of necessity, not choice.

While a gluten-free diet might seem like a solution to many modern health problems, it isn't always healthier if gluten-free products are processed and full of sugars or fats. Therefore, it's important to approach a gluten-free diet thoughtfully, based on solid nutritional knowledge.

Short Summary - My Daily Life

I have been on a gluten-free diet for 10 years. The beginnings were challenging because gluten-free products were just starting to enter the market back then. It took real effort to find suitable products, and cooking required more time and effort. Despite these challenges, I was determined to improve my health and continued my journey with gluten-free eating.

Today, I can't imagine consuming gluten, knowing the health effects it can cause. Most of my health issues have become a thing of the past. Over the years, I've learned how to plan meals and cook in a way that is quick, tasty, and healthy. All the meals in our home are now prepared gluten-free. My partner has also noticed a significant improvement in well-being after reducing wheat and gluten-containing products, and friends enjoy our meals with delight.

We have closely examined gluten, its role in the diet, and the challenges it poses for people with celiac disease or gluten intolerance. Now it's time to shift our focus to another important protein that plays a significant role in the daily diet of many people around the world—casein. This milk protein, like gluten, can be both beneficial and problematic for health. Let's take a closer look at casein, its properties, its impact on health, and its significance in various dietary contexts.

CHAPTER 5

Dairy - Casein - Milk Protein Under the Microscope

Casein is the main protein found in milk and dairy products, accounting for about 80% of all proteins in cow's milk. It is a source of essential amino acids necessary for the proper functioning of the body. However, much like gluten, it can cause health problems for some individuals.

Impact of Casein on Health

For most people, casein is a safe and valuable component of the diet. It provides high-quality protein, supports muscle growth and regeneration, and helps maintain healthy bones due to its calcium content. However, some individuals may experience negative reactions to casein, leading to various health issues.

Cow's Milk Protein Allergy (CMPA)

Cow's Milk Protein Allergy is one of the most common food allergies, particularly in children, though it can also occur in adults. Symptoms of this allergy can vary widely, from skin rashes and digestive problems such as diarrhea and vomiting, to hay fever, sinus issues, and breathing difficulties. In the most severe cases, anaphylaxis, a life-threatening condition, can occur. Individuals with CMPA must completely eliminate casein and other cow's milk proteins from their diet, which requires careful reading of labels and choosing appropriate substitute products.

Lactose Intolerance vs. Casein Intolerance

Lactose intolerance and casein intolerance are two distinct health issues that are often confused.

Lactose Intolerance:

Lactose intolerance results from a lack or deficiency of the enzyme lactase, which is essential for breaking down lactose, the sugar found in milk. Symptoms typically include bloating, abdominal pain, diarrhea, and gas. People with lactose intolerance can usually alleviate their symptoms by consuming lactose-free products, which provide the same nutritional benefits without causing digestive problems.

Casein Intolerance:

Casein intolerance involves an immune reaction to the casein protein found in milk. This can lead to inflammation, skin issues, and digestive problems. Unlike lactose intolerance, managing casein intolerance requires completely avoiding foods that contain casein, as the immune response can cause more severe and systemic symptoms.

Both issues necessitate eliminating certain components of milk from the diet. However, while lactose intolerance can often be managed with lactose-free products, casein intolerance requires avoiding all sources of casein.

Potential Impact on Chronic Diseases

The potential impact of casein on chronic diseases has become a subject of intensive scientific research. There are several hypotheses suggesting that regular consumption of casein may contribute to an increased risk of certain types of cancer, including colorectal, prostate, and breast cancer. Studies on this connection indicate that casein may stimulate the growth of cancer cells by affecting various metabolic and hormonal pathways, such as increasing the secretion of certain growth hormones.

Additionally, in the context of autoimmune diseases, casein is being analyzed for its potential role in provoking and sustaining inflammation in the body. These connections are being examined in diseases such as rheumatoid arthritis, multiple sclerosis, and inflammatory bowel diseases like Crohn's disease and ulcerative colitis.

Casein can provoke the immune system into undesirable reactions. This protein is difficult to digest—undigested fragments of these proteins remain in the body, and the immune system treats them as threats or "enemies." This, in turn, triggers a defensive response from the body to protect against the "intruder." This complex chain reaction can result in poor health and various health issues.

Why Casein Can Be Harmful? Milk and Antibiotics

Another concern related to casein is the presence of antibiotics in milk. In dairy farming, antibiotics are often used to prevent infections and diseases in cattle. Trace amounts of these substances can end up in milk and, consequently, in dairy products containing casein. Milk also contains residues of antibiotics, pesticides, herbicides, veterinary drugs, artificial fertilizers, synthetic preservatives, and food additives.

Consuming these products can lead to various health issues, including the development of antibiotic resistance, which poses a significant threat to public health.

Where Can You Find Casein?

Casein is present in many dairy products as well as some processed foods. The most common sources of casein include:

- **Milk and Cream:**
  Basic dairy products contain a significant amount of casein.

- **Yogurt and Kefir:**
  These fermented dairy products are also rich in casein.

- **Cheese:**
  Both hard and soft cheeses contain substantial amounts of casein, giving them their distinctive texture.

- **Ice Cream:**
  Traditional dairy ice cream is a source of casein.

- **Certain Processed Foods:**
  Casein can be added to various processed foods such as deli meats, prepared sauces, and even some bread to enhance texture and stability. Checking product labels is crucial for those with casein intolerance.

Casein Alternatives

For those looking to avoid casein, numerous alternatives are available that allow for a rich and balanced diet, regardless of the reasons for eliminating this protein.

Plant Proteins

The growing popularity of plant-based diets has led to a wide range of products based on plant proteins that can successfully replace casein:

- ✓ **Plant-Based Milks:**
  Alternatives to cow's milk, such as coconut, soy, almond, oat, and cashew milk, not only mimic the taste and texture of traditional milk but are often fortified with protein, calcium, vitamin D, and B12.

- ✓ **Plant Flours and Proteins:**
  Pea, soy, and hemp flours are excellent sources of protein for baking and cooking, enriching the diet with essential amino acids.

- ✓ **Nuts and Seeds:**
  Nuts and seeds are excellent sources of protein, healthy fats, and many essential vitamins and minerals that can support a healthy, casein-free diet.

Nuts:

- ✓ **Walnuts:** Rich in omega-3 fatty acids, magnesium, and vitamin E. They support heart and brain health.
- ✓ **Almonds:** High in protein, fiber, vitamin E, and magnesium. They promote bone and skin health.

- ✓ **Cashews:** A great source of iron, zinc, and protein. They support nervous and circulatory system health.
- ✓ **Pistachios:** Packed with fiber, protein, and vitamin B6. They help maintain eye and heart health.
- ✓ **Brazil Nuts:** Contain high amounts of selenium, which boosts the immune system and supports thyroid health.

Seeds:

- ✓ **Chia Seeds:** Rich in omega-3 fatty acids, fiber, and protein. They help maintain heart health and regulate blood sugar levels.
- ✓ **Flaxseeds:** Contain lignans, which have antioxidant properties, as well as fiber and omega-3 fatty acids.
- ✓ **Pumpkin Seeds:** High in magnesium, zinc, and healthy fats. They support prostate and heart health.
- ✓ **Sunflower Seeds:** Rich in vitamin E and selenium, helping to protect cells from oxidative damage.
- ✓ **Sesame Seeds:** Contain calcium, magnesium, and phosphorus, supporting bone health and the cardiovascular system.

Animal Proteins

For those who do not have issues with other animal proteins, there are plenty of options:

- ✓ **Eggs:**

  A versatile and excellent source of protein that can be easily incorporated into various dishes.

- ✓ **Fish:**

  Provides high-quality protein and is rich in omega-3 fatty acids, beneficial for heart health.

- ✓ **Meat:**
  Chicken and turkey are lean protein sources, while red meats like beef, venison, and lamb offer robust protein content.

When selecting substitute products, it's important to read labels carefully to ensure they don't contain added sugars, salts, or unhealthy fats that could negatively impact health. Casein-free products, especially those that are modified, may contain various additives to replicate the taste and texture of their traditional counterparts. Cheeses, butters, or desserts, although appealing in taste, should be consumed in moderation, following the 80/20 principle.

It's also advisable to consult with a dietitian or another qualified professional when making significant dietary changes to ensure the diet remains balanced and provides all necessary nutrients.

Short Summary - My Daily Life

In my daily diet, I also avoid products containing casein. The digestive issues I struggled with for years have disappeared, allowing me to enjoy a sense of well-being. Additionally, I have noticed a significant improvement in my skin. My partner's long-term sinus problems have also vanished. While I haven't been diagnosed with a casein allergy, I avoid dairy for better overall health. Occasionally, butter finds its way onto my gluten-free bread due to its nutritional value and nostalgic flavors from my childhood.

I remember the importance of balance and adhere to the 80/20 rule. I cook combining both gluten-free and casein-free diets, using ghee, which is free from casein. When shopping, I opt for plant-based yogurts and milk.

With the right approach and access to appropriate resources, a casein-free diet doesn't have to mean compromising on taste or meal quality. It can be an opportunity to explore new flavors and adopt a creative approach to cooking, resulting in health benefits and satisfaction from eating. Embracing a casein-free diet doesn't mean giving up favorite dishes. With the right knowledge and a bit of creativity, you can enjoy delicious and healthy meals that support your health and well-being.

Here is one of the recipes from my book: ***"Sugar, Gluten, and Dairy-Free Recipes".***

Recipe: Fettucine Alfredo with Mushrooms in Cream or Coconut Milk Sauce

Ingredients:

- 250g gluten-free fettucine pasta
- 250g mushrooms, sliced (any variety)
- 1 onion, finely chopped
- 2 cloves garlic, finely chopped
- 2 tbsp ghee or olive oil
- 1/2 cup white wine (optional)
- 1 cup plant-based cream or coconut milk
- 1/2 cup vegetable broth or pasta water
- 1/2 cup vegan parmesan (optional)

- 1 tsp dried oregano
- 1 tsp dried thyme
- Salt and pepper to taste
- Fresh parsley, chopped (for garnish)

Instructions:

1. **Cook the Pasta:**
   - Cook the gluten-free fettucine according to the package instructions until al dente.
   - Drain and set aside.

2. **Prepare the Mushroom Sauce:**
   - In a large skillet, heat the ghee or olive oil over medium heat.
   - Add the chopped onion and sauté until soft and slightly golden.
   - Add the garlic and sauté for another 1-2 minutes.
   - Add the mushrooms and cook until they soften and release their juices.
   - Optionally, add the white wine and cook until it evaporates.
   - Season with oregano, thyme, salt, and pepper to taste.
   - Add the plant-based cream or coconut milk and vegetable broth.
   - Bring to a boil, then reduce the heat and simmer for about 5-7 minutes until the sauce thickens.
   - Stir in the vegan parmesan, if using, and mix well.

3. **Combine the Pasta and Sauce:**
   - Add the cooked fettucine to the skillet with the mushroom sauce.

- o Mix thoroughly to ensure the pasta is evenly coated with the sauce.
- o Cook for an additional 1-2 minutes to combine flavors.

4. **Serve:**
   - o Plate the fettucine Alfredo with mushrooms.
   - o Garnish with fresh chopped parsley.
   - o Serve immediately.

We have taken a detailed look at the issue of allergies, particularly focusing on gluten and dairy, specifically casein. However, this is just the tip of the iceberg when it comes to food intolerances. It's important to remember that our bodies can have sensitivities to many other everyday foods. Examples include nuts, eggs—especially egg whites, soy, kiwi, pork, honey, chocolate, tomatoes, peppers, and even coffee. All of these can be strong allergens, leading not just to discomfort but also to serious health issues.

When we talk about coffee, it's worth mentioning that instant coffee is a product best avoided if we care about our health The process of its production involves the loss of many valuable ingredients and often includes the addition of chemicals that can negatively affect our body. In addition, the popular combination of coffee with sugar and milk becomes a real "inflammatory beverag" for the body - it promotes inflammation, which can lead to health problems. Instead of this harmful "mix", it is better to choose black coffee, e.g. Americano or espresso, which does not burden the body with additional ingredients. For people who particularly care about intestinal health, hormonal balance or reducing swelling, an even better option may be to replace coffee with green tea or matcha. These drinks are rich in antioxidants, have a stimulating effect, and at the same time support the body, preventing inflammation and promoting health.

Food intolerances and allergies can manifest in various ways, from subtle symptoms that are easy to overlook to severe reactions that significantly impact quality of life. This makes it crucial to be aware of what we eat and how our bodies react to different dietary components. Regular testing for food intolerances can be essential in uncovering hidden causes of poor health. With this knowledge, we can make more informed dietary choices, leading to better health and improved quality of life over time.

Understanding your body and its needs is one of the most important steps toward better well-being and health. Making conscious food choices based on solid knowledge can significantly affect how you feel each day.

After thoroughly discussing the health impacts of these products and the possibility of eliminating them from the diet, it's time to turn our attention to another critical aspect of our health—the impact of pesticides and herbicides on the body. Modern agriculture heavily relies on these chemicals, which greatly affects the quality of the food we consume. In the upcoming chapter, we will explore what pesticides and herbicides are, their uses, and the potential risks associated with their presence in our diet. We will also discuss how to avoid their negative effects by making informed food choices and opting for organic alternatives.

PART III

HIDDEN ENEMY STRONGHOLDS

CHAPTER 6

Chemistry on the Plate – Pesticides and Herbicides in Our Diet

Pesticides and herbicides are substances commonly used in modern agriculture to combat pests and weeds. While they effectively protect crops, they also pose risks to human health. In this chapter, we will delve into the impact of these chemicals on our diet and health, their presence in everyday food products, potential dangers, and strategies to minimize their effects on our lives.

Definition and Classification

Pesticides are substances used to combat pests such as insects (insecticides), fungi (fungicides), and rodents (rodenticides). They are designed to selectively target these threats, minimizing damage to crops. Herbicides, on the other hand, are a type of pesticide used to control unwanted plants, or weeds, which compete with crops for light, water, and nutrients.

Main Types of Chemicals Used in Pesticides and Their Impact on Health

Pesticides, despite their effectiveness, can pose risks to human and animal health. The three main groups of chemicals used in pesticides are organochlorine, organophosphate, and carbamate pesticides, each differing in their mechanisms of action and potential health effects.

Organochlorine Pesticides

Organochlorine pesticides, such as the infamous DDT, were widely used until the mid-20th century. However, their ability to persist in the environment has caused numerous ecological and health problems.

- **DDT (Dichlorodiphenyltrichloroethane)** can lead to hormonal disorders, an increased risk of cancer, and neurological developmental issues.
- **Lindane** is neurotoxic, carcinogenic, and disrupts hormonal balance.
- **Heptachlor** is potentially carcinogenic, affects the nervous system, and can cause developmental disorders.

Organophosphate Pesticides

Organophosphate pesticides are popular due to their effectiveness in disrupting the nervous system of insects. Unfortunately, similar mechanisms can negatively impact human health. Examples include:

- **Chlorpyrifos**, though banned in many places, is still available on the market. It is used to control pests in crops such as wheat, barley, canola, potatoes, cabbage, cauliflower, broccoli, plums, and strawberries. It can be a cause of obesity.

- **Malathion** causes respiratory disorders, headaches, and concentration problems.
- **Parathion** is highly toxic and can lead to death in cases of acute poisoning, showing neurotoxicity.

Carbamates

- **Carbaryl** can cause skin and mucous membrane irritation, dermatological issues, eye problems, and neurotoxic symptoms.
- **Aldicarb** is highly toxic; ingestion can lead to death, and it affects nervous system function.
- **Methomyl** causes neurotoxicity, respiratory disorders, and potential allergic reactions.

These are just some examples showing the importance of careful use to protect human health and the environment.

Risks Associated with Glyphosate

Glyphosate, known as the active ingredient in the popular herbicide Roundup, is widely used in agriculture, horticulture, and landscape management. Its presence in the environment raises significant health and ecological concerns. Scientific studies link glyphosate to diseases such as non-Hodgkin lymphoma, as well as hormonal and reproductive disorders.

Harmful Effects of Glyphosate on Humans

- ***IARC Classification***
  In 2015, the International Agency for Research on Cancer (IARC), part of the World Health Organization (WHO), classified glyphosate as "probably carcinogenic to humans" (Group 2A). This classification was based on "limited" evidence

of cancer in humans and "sufficient" evidence of cancer in experimental animals. IARC also found "strong" evidence of glyphosate's genotoxicity, both in its pure form and in commercial formulations.

- ***Epidemiological and Experimental Studies***
  IARC reviewed approximately 1,000 studies, including those on occupational exposure, such as among farmers. Epidemiological studies indicated an increased risk of non-Hodgkin lymphoma associated with exposure to glyphosate-containing herbicides. Additionally, animal studies showed that glyphosate causes tumors under laboratory conditions.

- ***Link to Endocrine and Reproductive Disorders***
  Recent studies suggest a connection between glyphosate and endocrine disorders, DNA damage, and reproductive issues. Experiments have shown that glyphosate can disrupt the endocrine system, leading to health problems such as infertility, miscarriages, and congenital disabilities in offspring. Furthermore, glyphosate has the potential to damage DNA, which can increase the risk of various cancers.

- ***Controversies and Differing Assessments***
  It is noteworthy that other regulatory agencies, such as the European Chemicals Agency (ECHA) and the U.S. Environmental Protection Agency (EPA), do not fully agree with the IARC's assessment. The EPA has concluded that glyphosate is "not likely" to be carcinogenic to humans based on a review of studies that the agency claims do not show sufficient evidence of glyphosate's carcinogenicity at typical exposure levels.

In summary, while there is evidence suggesting the carcinogenicity of glyphosate, significant debate and differing risk assessments exist among various organizations. Nonetheless, further research is essential to fully understand the long-term health effects of glyphosate and to ensure appropriate protective regulations for public health. Choosing organic and bio products minimizes the risk of exposure to these and other harmful chemicals, which is a step towards a healthier life and protecting our bodies from potentially harmful substances.

Exposure to Pesticides and Herbicides in the Daily Diet

Pesticides and herbicides are pervasive in many food products that regularly appear on our tables. Understanding how and why these substances are present in our food is crucial for making informed dietary decisions.

Penetration into the Food Chain

Pesticides can be found not only on the surface of plants but can also seep into the soil and water, leading to their accumulation throughout the food chain. Even food that comes from plants that seem "clean" can be contaminated.

Products at High Risk of Contamination

Certain products are more prone to pesticide contamination than others. Examples include:

- **Fruits and Vegetables with Soft Skins:**
  Apples, peaches, nectarines, strawberries, and grapes.

  Fruits and vegetables with soft skins are particularly susceptible to pesticide contamination because their thin skins do not provide an effective protective barrier. As a result, chemicals can easily penetrate the interior of the fruit, increasing the risk of pesticide consumption. Strawberries and grapes often appear on the "Dirty Dozen" list compiled by the Environmental Working Group (EWG), which highlights the most contaminated produce.

- **Leafy Vegetables:**
  Spinach and lettuce.

  Leafy vegetables, such as spinach and lettuce, have large surface areas that make them more prone to pesticide residues. The leaves of these vegetables are frequently sprayed with chemicals to protect them from insects and diseases, thereby increasing the risk of consuming pesticide residues.

- **Grains:**
  Wheat and corn.

  Grains like wheat and corn are widely cultivated and often treated with various pesticides and herbicides to enhance yields and control weeds. Due to their extensive use in food production, the presence of pesticides in grains can lead to contamination in numerous food products, such as bread, pasta, breakfast cereals, and other grain-based processed foods.

- **Processed Products:**
  Juices, sauces, and snacks.

  Processed products, such as fruit juices, sauces, and snacks, can contain pesticide residues that were present in the plant materials used during their cultivation. The processing often does not eliminate all chemical residues, meaning they can end up in the final product. For instance, fruit juices may contain pesticide residues from the fruits used in their production.

Minimizing Risk

To reduce exposure to pesticides and herbicides, consumers can take several steps:

⇨ **Choosing Organic Foods:**
Organic products are grown without synthetic pesticides and herbicides. Opting for organic fruits, vegetables, grains, and processed foods can significantly reduce the intake of harmful chemicals.

⇨ **Thorough Washing and Peeling:**
Wash fruits and vegetables under running water. Use a vegetable brush to scrub surfaces and consider peeling when appropriate. This can help remove residues from the skin of produce.

⇨ **Using Cleaning Solutions:**
Soak fruits and vegetables in solutions containing vinegar or baking soda. These solutions can help remove pesticide residues more effectively than water alone.

⇨ **Cooking:**
Cooking processes such as boiling, steaming, or blanching can reduce the levels of some pesticides. Ensure to cook food thoroughly to minimize chemical residues.

⇨ **Diversifying Diet**
Consume a wide variety of foods. Diversifying your diet can minimize the risk of consuming large amounts of a single type of pesticide. This approach helps spread the potential exposure across different food items, reducing the overall risk.

Education and Awareness

Raising awareness about the effects of pesticides and herbicides, including the use of glyphosate, and promoting healthy, sustainable agricultural practices are crucial for sustainable development. Educating farmers, consumers, and policymakers about safe alternatives to chemical herbicides can lead to better, more informed choices.

Short Summary - My Daily Life

In my daily life, I strive to purchase organic, bio, or locally farmed vegetables. Unfortunately, this is not always possible, so I make sure to clean thoroughly. I will discuss cleaning methods later in the book. While we shouldn't become overly obsessive, it is crucial to be cautious and aware of what we consume. A one-time consumption of widely available products may not significantly impact our health, but daily consumption can have side effects.

Understanding the risks associated with agricultural chemicals is key to a conscious approach to our health and diet. By choosing organic and bio products, we minimize the risk of exposure to harmful chemicals. Our informed decisions can improve the quality of our lives and protect the environment. Let's take care of our health by making wise and responsible choices.

However, this is not the only challenge we face in modern food production. In the following pages, we will examine another controversial technology that sparks much debate worldwide—genetically modified organisms (GMOs). Are GMOs a breakthrough in modern technology that can solve global food security issues, or do they conceal dangers that we are only beginning to uncover?

CHAPTER 7

GMO - Modern Technology or Threat?

In a world full of rapid technological advancements, the genetic modification of plants and animals stirs strong emotions and discussions. Genetically modified organisms (GMOs) are those whose DNA has been altered in ways that do not occur naturally, often by introducing genes from another species. This approach aims to produce plants that are more resistant to diseases, pests, and even climate change. But is GMO merely a modern technology serving a better future, or a potential threat to health and the environment?

What are GMOs?

GMOs, or genetically modified organisms, are products created through genetic engineering. This technology allows scientists to selectively add desired traits to plants or animals, such as increased resistance to diseases or improved nutritional value.

Examples of GMO foods include:

- **Soybeans:**
  Enhanced resistance to herbicides and pests. Commonly used in soybean oil, tofu, and various forms of textured vegetable protein.

- **Corn:**
  Resistant to herbicides and pests, reducing the need for chemical crop protection. Used in corn syrup, cornmeal, and as animal feed.

- **Cotton:**
  Used in the production of cottonseed oil, which is utilized in the food industry.

- **Potatoes:**
  Genetically modified to reduce browning and acrylamide production during frying.

- **Papayas:**
  Engineered to resist the papaya ringspot virus, saving crops from disease.

- **Wheat:**
  One of the most important grains worldwide, with genetic modifications raising particular controversy. There are concerns that modified wheat may lead to new allergies or intolerances and decrease the genetic diversity of traditional wheat varieties.

GMO Animals: A Threat?

The FDA has approved the sale of AquAdvantage salmon, genetically modified to grow twice as fast as conventional salmon. These fish are raised in contained, artificial ponds to minimize the risk of escaping into the wild. Most of the fish are sterile females, preventing them from reproducing if they do escape.

Opponents of GMOs worry that if these modified salmon were to escape into the ocean, they could outcompete natural species. Some food distributors have already announced they will not carry GMO salmon in their stores, even though U.S. law does not require GMO products to be labeled as such.

GMO Supporters: Benefits and Doubts

Proponents of GMOs emphasize the numerous advantages of this technology, claiming that the genetic modification of plants and animals can lead to significant benefits for both agriculture and consumers. But are these arguments as clear-cut as they seem? Let's examine some of them:

Increased Crop Yields

Supporters of GMOs argue that genetically modified plants can produce higher yields, which is crucial given the growing global population. These plants can be more resistant to pests, diseases, and adverse climatic conditions, theoretically leading to fewer losses and greater food production.

However, do these promises always hold true? In reality, some studies suggest that GMO yields may not be higher than those of traditional varieties, and the economic benefits often depend on specific local conditions and the technology used by farmers. For example, research conducted by the Union of Concerned Scientists indicates that significant yield increases are not always achieved through the use of GMOs.

Reduced Use of Pesticides

One of the key arguments for GMOs is that they can reduce the need for chemical pesticides. For instance, genetically modified plants designed to produce their own pest protection can theoretically reduce the amount of pesticides needed.

But is it really that simple? Critics point out that the long-term use of GMO crops can lead to the development of superweeds and superbugs that are resistant to herbicides and pesticides, ultimately requiring the use of even stronger chemicals. Reports from Environmental Sciences Europe show an increase in pesticide use in the USA as a result of GMO cultivation.

Improved Nutritional Value

Some genetically modified food products have been designed to increase their nutritional value. An example is "Golden Rice," which has been enriched with vitamin A to help combat vitamin A deficiencies in developing countries.

Do these modifications always deliver the expected health benefits? There are concerns that such modifications could lead to unforeseen side effects or interactions with other dietary components. Research published in Nature highlights various aspects of this issue and shows that the implementation of Golden Rice has faced numerous challenges.

Better Tolerance to Variable Climate Conditions

GMO plants can be engineered to better withstand extreme conditions, such as drought or excessive moisture, which is increasingly important in the face of climate change. However, are these solutions always effective? Some researchers point out that genetic modifications alone may not be sufficient to mitigate the impacts of climate change, and that more comprehensive approaches to agricultural management are needed. Studies in Frontiers in Plant Science emphasize that while GMOs can play a role, they are not the sole solution.

Health Issues Related to GMOs

While proponents of GMOs point to many potential benefits, it is essential to approach these promises with caution. The reality is more complex, and some advantages may be less clear-cut than they appear at first glance. The future of GMO technology in agriculture depends on further research and debates about its long-term effects on human health and the environment. Remember, genetically engineered food is not natural for our bodies, which may pose a health risk because our bodies do not have the necessary enzymes to process it.

One of the most frequently discussed aspects of GMO food is the potential health issues. While this technology promises many benefits, such as higher yields and pest resistance, concerns about its impact on human health spark debates among scientists and consumers alike.

➢ ***Allergies and Food Sensitivity:***
One major concern is the possibility that genetically modified food may cause allergies. Genetic modifications can introduce new proteins into plants, which theoretically can increase the risk of allergic reactions, especially if these proteins are derived from known allergens.

➢ ***Long-Term Health Effects:***
Although many studies suggest that GMOs are safe, there are relatively few long-term studies on their impact on human health. Critics argue that without long-term studies, it is difficult to definitively state that GMO foods do not lead to chronic diseases, reproductive problems, or other health issues. Toxicity studies on animals with some types of GMO foods have shown that they can

negatively affect the liver, pancreas, kidneys, and biochemical blood parameters.

- ***Uncertainty and Regulations:***
  Many countries have implemented stringent regulations on GMO labeling, allowing consumers to make informed choices. However, differences in international regulations can affect how GMO foods are tested, evaluated, and labeled before they hit the market.

In summary, while GMOs have the potential to offer significant benefits, it is essential to consider the possible health risks and ensure rigorous testing and regulation to safeguard public health.

Environmental Impact

Genetic modification of plants has clear advantages, such as increased pest resistance and better tolerance to adverse environmental conditions, which translate to higher yields. However, the introduction of genetically modified organisms (GMOs) into the natural environment also raises significant concerns about the potential impact on biodiversity and ecosystem stability.

- ***Gene Transfer:***
  Genes transferred to GMO crops can infiltrate wild populations, leading to the emergence of "superweeds" that exhibit resistance to herbicides. This gene transfer can force farmers to use even stronger and potentially more harmful chemicals, negatively affecting human health and the environment.

- ***Reduction in Biodiversity:***
  GMO monocultures can lead to a loss of biodiversity, which limits

ecosystems' ability to adapt to climate change and other environmental stresses.

Ethical and Economic Consequences:

The ethical and economic issues associated with GMOs are highly controversial:

- ***Market Monopolization of Seeds:***
  Large biotech corporations often hold patents on genetically modified seeds, increasing farmers' dependency on these companies and potentially raising production costs. These patents restrict farmers from saving and replanting seeds from their crops, forcing them to purchase new seeds each year. This dependency is particularly problematic in developing regions where it can exacerbate economic challenges for small-scale farmers.

- ***Limitation of Innovation:***
  The concentration of seed control within a few large companies can stifle innovation in sustainable agriculture. This monopolization not only affects farmers' rights but also has implications for global food security. Ensuring a diverse and competitive market is crucial for fostering innovation and sustainable practices in agriculture.

In the context of rapidly advancing technology, GMOs present promising opportunities to improve agricultural efficiency and reduce its environmental impact. However, from the perspectives of public health, environmental protection, and ethics, there are numerous questions and controversies that require further research and debate. The future of GMOs hinges on finding a balance between innovation and responsibility, ensuring that the benefits are widely distributed while minimizing risks to health and the environment. Remember, genetically modified food is artificial, and our bodies may not recognize it as a desirable component, making it wise to exclude it from our diets.

Short Summary - My Daily Life

Being aware of the potential side effects of GMO foods, I avoid them in my daily life. My shopping choices are carefully considered, and I always opt for natural and organic products to avoid the risks associated with genetic modifications. This approach helps me safeguard the health of myself and my loved ones, ensuring our daily well-being and safety.

Having explored the controversies surrounding genetically modified food and its impact on our health and the environment, we now turn our attention to another critical aspect of the modern diet – the meat industry. What are the consequences of mass meat production for our health, animals, and the planet? Is sustainable animal farming possible? You will find answers to these questions in the next chapter.

CHAPTER 8

The Meat Industry Under the Microscope

The meat industry plays a significant role in our daily lives, providing products that grace our tables worldwide. However, meat production involves much more than just processing — it encompasses complex issues related to environmental impact, human health, and animal welfare. In this chapter, we will closely examine these aspects, seeking to understand what actions can be taken to make meat production more sustainable and ethical.

The Impact of the Meat Industry on Health

The meat industry plays a significant role in the diet of many individuals, providing protein and other essential nutrients. However, the methods of meat production, including the use of antibiotics, growth hormones, and preservatives, raise concerns about their impact on human health and the conditions in which animals are raised.

Antibiotics, Preservatives, and Farming Methods

- ***Antibiotics and Growth Hormones:***

  The use of antibiotics in livestock farming is widespread, primarily to prevent diseases among farm animals and to promote faster growth. While these practices can enhance production efficiency, they pose significant public health risks, particularly concerning the development of antibiotic resistance. Antibiotic-resistant bacteria can transfer from farms to humans, making some infections more difficult to treat.

  Growth hormones, although banned in many countries like those in the European Union, are still used in other regions to accelerate animal growth. Residues of these substances in meat can affect human hormonal balance, contributing to various health issues.

- ***Preservatives in Meat:***

  Processed meats often contain preservatives to extend shelf life and improve flavor and appearance. Substances such as nitrates and nitrites, used in sausages and bacon, can transform into nitrosamines in the body, which are potentially carcinogenic. Consuming large amounts of processed meat has been linked to a higher risk of heart disease, type 2 diabetes, and certain types of cancer, including colorectal cancer.

- ***Farming Conditions:***

  The conditions in which animals are raised also impact the quality and safety of meat. Animals raised in poor conditions, often under stress, are more susceptible to diseases, leading to increased antibiotic use. Moreover, stress and poor treatment of animals can alter the biochemical composition of meat, affecting its nutritional properties and taste.

Understanding the methods and implications of meat production is crucial for making informed dietary choices. By being aware of the potential health risks associated with antibiotics, preservatives, and poor farming conditions, consumers can better navigate their options for healthier, more sustainable meat consumption.

The Meat Industry and the Environment

The meat industry significantly impacts our planet by emitting methane and other greenhouse gases, contributing to global warming. Intensive livestock farming consumes vast amounts of water and feed, leading to soil degradation and water pollution from animal waste containing nitrates and pathogens. To mitigate this negative impact, it is crucial to reduce meat consumption and support ecological production methods.

Most Contaminated and Healthiest Meat

Meat from conventional farming, where antibiotics and hormones are used, as well as processed meat, are considered the most contaminated. Pork and chicken, the most commonly purchased types of meat, often contain antibiotic and hormone residues, which further increase health risks for consumers. Conversely, organic meat from animals raised in more natural conditions, without artificial hormones and with minimal or no antibiotic use, is considered a healthier option.

Conscious Choices

Making informed choices is essential. Prefer meat from certified organic sources, opt for beef, lamb, venison, or turkey, support local farmers using sustainable farming practices, and reduce the consumption of processed meat. These actions can contribute to better health and a lesser environmental burden.

Short Summary - My Daily Life

Knowing how the meat industry operates, I place a great deal of importance on the quality of the meat I consume. I primarily purchase organic products and those from local farmers. I am aware that these animals are not raised in harsh conditions and are properly fed, without being pumped full of antibiotics and modified feeds to quickly gain weight.

By choosing sustainable sources of meat, supporting ethical farming practices, and exploring alternatives, each of us can contribute to changes that benefit both us and future generations. Understanding the impact of the meat industry on our planet and our health is another step towards making informed decisions that can lead to a healthier and more sustainable lifestyle.

Next, we will delve into the topic of heavy metals in food, discovering how substances like lead, mercury, and cadmium can enter our diets and their effects on health. We will explore sources of contamination, potential health impacts, and strategies we can use to minimize risk and protect ourselves and our loved ones from these dangerous substances.

CHAPTER 9

Heavy Metals in Food – Hidden Danger on Our Plates

In today's world, where technology and industry permeate almost every aspect of our lives, exposure to heavy metals has become a serious health concern. Substances such as lead, mercury, cadmium, and arsenic can find their way into our meals, posing long-term health risks.

The Impact of Heavy Metals on Health: What You Need to Know

Heavy metals in our diet can lead to a range of severe health problems, affecting both adults and children. Here's an overview of some key heavy metals and their effects on health:

- **Lead:**
  Long-term exposure to lead can result in poisoning that affects the nervous system, causing concentration problems, headaches, and in severe cases, brain damage. In children, it can disrupt neurological development and lower IQ levels. Lead can also cause kidney issues and cardiovascular problems.

- **Mercury:**
  Found mainly in fish and seafood, mercury can cause neurological disorders and kidney damage. In pregnant women, mercury exposure can affect fetal development, leading to birth defects and developmental delays. Mercury can also impact cognitive functions and cardiovascular health.

- **Cadmium:**
  Long-term exposure to cadmium, often present in grains and leafy vegetables, can lead to kidney problems, osteoporosis, and other bone disorders. Cadmium is also classified as a potential human carcinogen. It can cause respiratory issues and increase the risk of lung cancer.

- **Arsenic:**
  Arsenic can be present in drinking water and certain foods like rice. Chronic exposure to arsenic can lead to cancer, cardiovascular diseases, and skin problems. Children and pregnant women are particularly vulnerable to the health risks associated with arsenic.

Exposure to heavy metals such as lead, mercury, cadmium, and arsenic poses a significant public health risk. Prolonged exposure to these substances can result in various severe health issues, including neurological disorders, cardiovascular diseases, kidney damage, and different types of cancer. Awareness of the sources of these metals and taking appropriate steps to minimize exposure is crucial for protecting health.

How Do Heavy Metals Get Into Our Food?

Heavy metals can enter our food in various ways:

- ***Soil Contamination:***
  Lead, once commonly used in gasoline and paints, can linger in the soil for decades, contaminating crops.

- ***Water Pollution:***
  Mercury, released into waters from industrial processes, accumulates in fish and seafood, especially in predatory species like tuna and shark.

- ***Fertilizers:***
  Cadmium often comes from phosphate fertilizers used in agriculture.

Most Contaminated Products

Products rich in heavy metals are usually those that accumulate these substances from soil or water. High concentrations of heavy metals are often found in:

- **Seafood:**
  Particularly in large predatory fish like tuna, swordfish, and shark, which accumulate mercury in their tissues. Some seafood can also contain organic forms of arsenic, which are less toxic but still contribute to overall exposure.

- **Leafy Vegetables:**
  Such as spinach and lettuce, which can accumulate cadmium from contaminated soils.

- **Grains:**
  Cadmium can be present due to soil contamination from phosphate fertilizers.

- **Rice and Rice Products:**
  Rice grown in flooded fields can contain high levels of arsenic, absorbed from the water and soil.

How Can We Minimize the Risk?

⇨ **Choose organic products:**
Organic products are grown without the use of synthetic fertilizers and pesticides, which reduces the risk of heavy metal contamination.

⇨ **Thoroughly wash fruits and vegetables:**
Washing under running water can help remove some external contaminants. Employ additional cleaning methods like a baking soda and apple cider vinegar solution or ozonation—these topics will be explored in more detail later in the book.

⇨ **Avoid excessive consumption of high food chain fish:**
Fish such as tuna, swordfish, shark, and king mackerel often accumulate higher amounts of mercury due to their long lifespan and predatory nature.

Which Fish Are Safer?

To minimize the risk of mercury exposure, consider these alternatives:

✓ **Sardines:**
Small, short-lived fish like sardines are much less likely to accumulate mercury and are rich in omega-3 fatty acids.

- ✓ **Trout:**
  Especially farmed trout, which are usually raised in controlled conditions, generally have low mercury levels.

- ✓ **Cod:**
  Atlantic and Pacific cod have lower mercury levels due to their diets mainly consisting of small invertebrates.

- ✓ **Salmon:**
  Both wild and farmed salmon are considered low in mercury.

- ✓ **Tilapia:**
  With a low position in the food chain, tilapia typically contains low mercury levels.

Practical Tips for Choosing Fish

- ⇨ **Check Labels:**
  Pay attention to the source of the fish. Wild-caught fish can have different mercury levels compared to farm-raised fish, depending on their natural environment. Choose reliable sources and consider using an ozonator for additional purification.

- ⇨ **Diversify Your Diet:**
  Eating a variety of fish not only helps diversify nutrient intake but also reduces the risk of mercury exposure.

- ⇨ **Avoid Frequent Consumption of Large Predatory Fish:**
  Limiting the consumption of fish like shark, swordfish, and large tuna can significantly reduce mercury intake.

Supporting Sustainable Practices

Supporting local farmers who use sustainable practices can help reduce the use of dangerous chemicals in agriculture. Understanding the impact of heavy metals on our health and the environment is crucial for making informed choices that are healthier for us and our families. Making conscious decisions about what we eat not only improves our health but also contributes to protecting the environment from further contamination.

Short Summary - My Daily Life

Understanding how heavy metals affect our bodies and the health consequences they cause, I cleanse my food using methods mentioned earlier. Additionally, I avoid products with high concentrations of heavy metals, such as grains and tuna, and consume seafood very sparingly. I try to buy vegetables from trusted sources to minimize exposure to harmful substances. I also use supplements to help detoxify my body and remove heavy metals, but more on that later in the book.

In the next chapter, we will explore another important aspect of modern diets: the contrast between fast food and slow food. We will consider the health and social benefits of slowing down our eating habits and adopting a more mindful approach to meals, as well as the dangers associated with fast food consumption.

Get ready for a fascinating journey through the world of food, where we will discover how our daily choices can impact our health, well-being, and the future of our planet.

CHAPTER 10

Fast Food vs. Slow Food - The Battle for Our Health

In today's fast-paced world, the choice between fast food and slow food is becoming increasingly important for our health and well-being. What we put on our plates directly affects not only our weight but also our overall health, mood, and even lifespan.

Fast food—tempting with its convenience and quick service—is often a symbol of an unhealthy diet. These meals are typically high in calories, saturated fats, sugars, and salt, while lacking essential nutrients such as fiber, vitamins, and minerals. Regular consumption of fast food can lead to numerous health problems, including obesity, type 2 diabetes, heart disease, and other chronic illnesses.

On the other hand, slow food encourages a return to our roots—promoting the consumption of local, seasonal products, home cooking, and paying greater attention to what we eat. The philosophy of slow food is based on the idea that food should be a source of pleasure, should respect the natural environment, and support local economies. A diet based on slow food principles is rich in fresh fruits and vegetables, whole grains, and healthy fats, which promotes long-term health and helps prevent many lifestyle-related diseases.

Why Choose Slow Food?

Choosing slow food is not just a return to our roots but also an investment in our health and the environment. Here's why incorporating the philosophy of slow food into your life is worthwhile:

Healthier ingredients are the foundation of the slow food philosophy, emphasizing the importance of natural, unprocessed products in our diet. Here are the health benefits of choosing such products, along with examples of dishes and products that align with this idea:

⇨ **More Nutrients:**
Unprocessed foods usually retain more vitamins, minerals, and other essential nutrients often lost during processing. For instance, fresh fruits and vegetables like broccoli or blueberries are rich in antioxidants that support our immune system.

⇨ **No Artificial Additives:**
By choosing slow food products, we avoid preservatives, artificial colors, and flavor enhancers commonly found in processed foods. This makes our diet cleaner and more natural.

Examples of Slow Food Dishes and Products

✓ **Salad with Fresh Vegetables and Blueberries:**
A simple yet incredibly nutritious meal, rich in vitamins and fiber.

- ✓ **Baked Cod with Herbs:**
  Fish prepared simply and served with greens, providing high-quality protein and healthy omega-3 fats.

- ✓ **Homemade Sourdough Bread:**
  Baked from whole grain flour without additives that improve texture or preservatives found in commercial breads.

- ✓ **Homemade Fermented Foods:**
  Such as sauerkraut or pickles, these are natural sources of probiotics that support gut health.

By choosing these and similar products, we can enjoy not only the taste of real food but also the health benefits of a diet based on unprocessed, natural ingredients.

Challenges Associated with Fast Food

Despite the convenience fast food offers, it's important to remember the negative aspects of such a diet, including high levels of unhealthy fats and sugars. Frequent consumption of fast food can lead to weight gain and associated health issues. The modern food landscape offers a wide range of fast foods that, despite their convenience and affordability, pose significant health challenges. Here are some examples of popular fast foods that can negatively impact health:

- **Burgers:**
  While commonly considered a quick and tasty meal, burgers often contain high levels of saturated fats and calories, contributing to weight gain and cardiovascular issues.

- **French Fries:**
  A popular side dish for many fast foods, fries are usually fried in oil, increasing their content of unhealthy trans fats and calories.

- **Fizzy drinks:**
  Often served as part of a fast food meal, sodas are loaded with sugars, which can contribute to the development of type 2 diabetes, tooth decay, and other health problems.

- **Pizza:**
  Although it can be made in healthier versions, most commercially available pizzas are high in saturated fats, salt, and calories, making them a less healthy choice.

- **Sweet Snacks:**
  Cookies, cakes, and other sweet treats, often found in fast food outlets, are highly processed and contain large amounts of sugars and trans fats.

- **Frozen Ready Meals:**
  Increasingly common on our tables due to their easy availability and convenience. Rich in trans fats and sugars, these meals are often based on modified products, prepared at high temperatures, and lack significant nutritional value.

Impact on Physical and Mental Health

A diet based on fast foods can significantly affect our physical health. High intake of saturated fats, sugars, and salt can lead to obesity, type 2 diabetes, hypertension, and heart disease. Fast food also often contains low amounts of fiber, which can cause digestive issues and increase the risk of colorectal cancer.

A fast food diet can also impact our mental health. Studies indicate that high consumption of processed foods is associated with an increased risk of depression and anxiety. This phenomenon may be linked to the effects of a poor diet on blood sugar levels and body inflammation, which can influence brain function. Research suggests that a diet high in processed foods correlates with a higher risk of depression and anxiety.

The Importance of Conscious Choices

Despite these challenges, we don't have to entirely give up the convenience that fast food offers. The key is to make conscious choices for healthier options, such as opting for salads, grilled instead of fried dishes, or sugar-free beverages. Additionally, incorporating more home-cooked meals into our diet provides complete control over ingredients and cooking methods.

Examples of Healthier Alternatives:

- ⇨ **Instead of fast food fries:** Baked potatoes with olive oil and herbs.
- ⇨ **Instead of a hamburger:** Lentil burger with whole grain or gluten-free bun and fresh vegetables.
- ⇨ **Instead of soda:** Water with lemon and mint or homemade fruit juice.
- ⇨ **Instead of processed pizza:** Homemade pizza with a cauliflower or gluten-free crust, topped with vegetables.
- ⇨ **Instead of sugary snacks:** Fresh fruits, nuts, or natural yogurt with honey.

Choosing between fast food and slow food is more than just deciding what to eat for dinner. While fast food may be a tempting solution for a quick meal, it's important to remember its potential negative impact on our physical and mental health. This decision is about adopting a lifestyle that can affect our health, environment, and community. By opting for conscious, healthy food choices, we can not only improve our own health but also contribute to creating a healthier future for generations to come.

Short Summary - My Daily Life

My diet mainly revolves around the slow food method. I prefer a variety of salads and vegetables, paired with high-quality meat, fish, and eggs. Even when dining out, I opt for these choices since they are now readily available in most restaurants. I consciously avoid places like McDonald's, Pizza Hut, Burger King, and similar establishments, as I believe they do not offer real, nutritious food.

A few times a year, following the 80/20 rule, I indulge in gluten-free fish and chips, especially when tempted by the seaside aroma, or a real lamb kebab with a side of salads and vegetables. We must remember that we are only human, and excessive restriction can lead to chronic stress on a subconscious level. Therefore, it's sometimes worthwhile to allow yourself a bit of "indulgence" and enjoy a "better version" of a less healthy meal, especially in pleasant surroundings and good company.

Balance and awareness are key. My dietary choices aim not only at physical health but also at maintaining mental balance and enjoyment in eating.

PART IV

WATER - THE SOURCE OF LIFE

CHAPTER 11

Water - The Source of Life, The Source of Threats

The Importance of Water for Human Health

Water makes up about 60% of an adult's body weight, making it an essential component for the proper functioning of every system in our body. From transporting nutrients and maintaining electrolyte balance to regulating body temperature and supporting digestive processes, water is crucial for health and life.

The Role of Water in Diet and Nutrition

Water is not only a fundamental component of every cell in our body but also a crucial element for the proper functioning of the entire organism. Its role in diet and nutrition is invaluable, and optimal hydration is the foundation of a healthy lifestyle. Water plays a vital role in the body through:

⇨ **Supporting Metabolism:**
Proper hydration is essential for efficient metabolism. Water participates in metabolic processes and helps convert nutrients into energy.

⇨ **Removing Toxins:**

Water is necessary for eliminating waste and toxins from the body. It aids the kidneys in filtering and removing unnecessary substances through urine.

⇨ **Transporting Nutrients and Eliminating Toxins:**

Water enables the transport of nutrients to cells and the removal of metabolic waste products and toxins. Proper hydration ensures efficient kidney function, which is responsible for filtering and removing waste from the body.

⇨ **Maintaining Electrolyte Balance:**

Water helps maintain electrolyte balance, crucial for many life functions, including heart and muscle activity. Adequate hydration keeps electrolytes like sodium, potassium, and magnesium within optimal levels.

⇨ **Regulating Body Temperature:**

Proper hydration is necessary for regulating body temperature. Water is involved in the sweating process, allowing for cooling and preventing overheating, especially in warm conditions or during physical exertion. When body temperature rises, the body secretes sweat, which cools the skin as it evaporates, lowering body temperature.

⇨ **Supporting Digestion and Metabolism:**

Water is essential for proper digestion and nutrient absorption. It aids in breaking down food, facilitating its movement through the digestive tract, and preventing constipation.

⇨ **Impact on Skin Health and Appearance:**
Adequate hydration helps maintain skin elasticity, preventing dryness and the formation of wrinkles. Water also helps maintain a healthy, radiant skin appearance.

Understanding these aspects highlights how crucial water is for our health. To maintain optimal hydration, it is recommended to drink an adequate amount of water each day—usually about 2-3 liters, depending on individual needs, climatic conditions, and physical activity levels.

Water Pollution and Its Impact on Health

Water pollution is one of the greatest public health challenges globally. The sources of contamination are varied and include industrial, agricultural activities, and environmental pollution. Water contaminated with heavy metals, pesticides, microorganisms, and other harmful substances can lead to a range of health problems.

- **Heavy Metals:**
  Heavy metals such as lead, mercury, and cadmium can infiltrate groundwater and surface water due to industrial mining activities, metal processing, and air pollution. Consumption of water contaminated with heavy metals can result in neurological diseases, developmental disorders in children, kidney problems, and an increased risk of certain cancers.

- **Pesticides**
  Residues of pesticides used in agriculture can enter water bodies through surface runoff. Drinking water contaminated with pesticides can cause nervous system issues, hormonal imbalances, liver damage, and reproductive problems.

- **Microorganisms:**
  Bacteria, viruses, and parasites are common water contaminants, particularly in areas lacking proper sanitation and hygiene infrastructure. Waterborne diseases such as cholera, diarrhea, and hepatitis A often result from consuming contaminated water.

- **Chemical Contaminants:**
  Industrial chemical waste, including PFAS (poly- and perfluoroalkyl substances), which are challenging to remove and have long-term environmental impacts, can pollute water. These substances can affect the immune and reproductive systems, lead to thyroid diseases, and cause other health disorders.

Understanding the various sources and types of water pollution highlights the importance of ensuring safe drinking water to protect public health. Effective measures to prevent water contamination and proper treatment of polluted water are crucial steps in mitigating these health risks.

Methods of Water Purification and Treatment

In response to growing concerns about drinking water quality, various filtration and treatment methods have gained popularity. These techniques effectively eliminate many contaminants, ensuring safe and clean water for domestic use. Here are some of the most popular methods:

⇨ **Carbon Filtration**
Carbon filters are widely used due to their ability to remove chlorine, pesticides, and certain organic compounds by adsorbing contaminants onto activated carbon. However, they are not fully effective against heavy metals or all microorganisms.

⇨ **Reverse Osmosis**

Reverse osmosis systems use a semi-permeable membrane to remove almost all types of contaminants, including salts, bacteria, and viruses. This is one of the most effective water purification methods.

⇨ **Distillation**

Distillation involves boiling water and then condensing the steam, resulting in very pure water. It is highly effective at removing heavy metals, minerals, and other contaminants, but the process is time-consuming and energy-intensive.

⇨ **Ceramic Filtration**

Ceramic filters are effective at eliminating bacteria, protozoa, and other particles due to the microscopic pores in the ceramic. However, they are not effective against dissolved chemical contaminants.

⇨ **Ultraviolet Filtration**

UV water purification uses ultraviolet light to destroy the DNA of bacteria and viruses, making it effective against these microorganisms. This method does not remove chemical contaminants or heavy metals.

⇨ **Ion Exchange Systems**

Ion exchange filters, often used for water softening, work by exchanging harmful mineral ions with less harmful ones. They can be used to remove radon, heavy metals, and certain other contaminants.

Each of these methods has its advantages and limitations, making it important to tailor the choice of system to specific needs, the quality of available water, and financial capabilities. Regular monitoring of the chosen filtration system's effectiveness and adjusting it to changing conditions and new water quality standards is also crucial.

Bottled Water vs. Tap Water – Risks and Benefits

Choosing between bottled water and tap water is a common dilemma for many people, especially those striving to make informed decisions about their health, the environment, and their budget. Here is an overview of the main advantages and disadvantages of both sources of water:

Advantages and Disadvantages of Bottled Water:

Bottled water is easily accessible and portable, making it a convenient choice for travel or situations where access to fresh tap water is limited. It can be found in most stores, gas stations, and vending machines, ensuring that hydration is always within reach when needed. Opt for water in glass bottles if possible, to protect yourself from harmful chemicals found in plastic. Another option is to carry your own filtered water when leaving home, ensuring you always have clean water on hand when you're thirsty.

Advantages and Disadvantages of Tap Water:

Drinking tap water can significantly reduce the costs associated with hydration, especially in regions where tap water is safe and readily available. Using tap water minimizes the need for plastic bottles, reducing waste and pollution. Tap water in many countries is subject to strict sanitary regulations, ensuring high quality and safety. In some areas, tap water may be contaminated with heavy metals, pesticides, or other harmful substances, which might require additional filtering. Additionally, tap water can sometimes have an unpleasant taste or smell, such as from chlorination, which may deter people from drinking it.

Installing a home water filter ensures that you are hydrating with good quality water that tastes pleasant.

Tips for Optimal Hydration

⇨ **Monitor Your Water Intake:**
Adults should aim to drink about 8-10 glasses of water daily, but individual needs may vary depending on age, weight, physical activity, and climate conditions.

⇨ **Listen to Your Body's Signals:**
Thirst is a natural signal that your body needs water. Don't ignore this signal, but also try to drink water regularly throughout the day before you even feel thirsty. Often, we confuse signals and reach for something to eat, especially sugary snacks, when we are actually just dehydrated. This not only fails to address the problem but also adds unnecessary calories to our diet. Regular hydration is key to maintaining good health and proper body function.

⇨ **Drink Water Before Meals:**
Drinking water before meals can help you feel full and prevent overeating, which is particularly important for weight control.

⇨ **Avoid Dehydration:**
Signs of dehydration include fatigue, dry mouth, headache, and dizziness. Regular water consumption helps avoid these unpleasant symptoms.

⇨ **Choose Water Over Sugary Drinks:**
Water is the best choice for hydration. Avoiding sugary drinks, juices, and energy drinks helps prevent the intake of unnecessary calories and sugars.

Hydrogen Water - Elixir of Life?

In recent years, hydrogen water has gained popularity as a potentially beneficial health drink. Hydrogen water is simply regular water infused with hydrogen molecules (H2), which are believed to act as powerful antioxidants, combating free radicals in the body.

Health Benefits of Hydrogen Water

✓ **Antioxidant Properties:**
Hydrogen acts as an antioxidant, neutralizing harmful free radicals that can cause cellular damage and lead to inflammation.

✓ **Reduction of Inflammation:**
Studies suggest that hydrogen water may help reduce inflammation, beneficial for individuals with inflammatory conditions such as arthritis.

✓ **Improved Metabolism:**
Regular consumption of hydrogen water can support metabolism and contribute to overall health improvement.

✓ **Cardiovascular Support:**
Hydrogen water may aid cardiovascular health by helping regulate blood pressure and improving blood vessel function.

- ✓ **Increased Energy and Physical Performance:** Some research indicates that hydrogen water can boost energy levels and enhance physical performance, which is advantageous for athletes and physically active individuals.

Understanding the impact of water on our health and being aware of the dangers associated with water contamination are crucial for making informed hydration decisions. By choosing appropriate water purification methods, avoiding excessive consumption of bottled water in plastic, and maintaining regular hydration, we can significantly enhance our quality of life and well-being.

Short Summary - My Daily Life

Water is the foundation of life, and its quality and availability have a direct impact on our well-being. Every organ in our body needs water. Do you know the water content of our organs? Here it is: brain – 75%, lungs – 80%, muscles – 75%, kidneys – 80%, eyes – 80%, skin – 75%, bones – 25%, and fat tissue – 10%. Drinking the right amount of water is essential to our diet.

At home, I have a multi-stage water filter installed. When I want to drink sparkling water, I make it myself using a Soda Stream device. The quality of the water is incomparable. When I'm out, I bring my own water or buy water in glass bottles. In extreme cases, I opt for the lesser evil and choose water in plastic bottles to avoid dehydration. We live in times where we can do so much for our bodies by minimizing exposure to contaminated and polluted products.

Additionally, I drink hydrogen water, which I also make myself using a special bottle. I pay attention to the amount of water I drink throughout the day because life has repeatedly shown me that a lack of it causes fatigue and poor well-being on many levels – from digestive problems and headaches to constipation and swelling.

I add a pinch of salt, lemon juice, mint, a slice of ginger, or cucumber to my water, making electrolytes that ensure proper hydration.

I start every day with a glass of warm water with lemon. It's a simple but highly effective way to awaken my body and prepare it for the new day. The warm water gently stimulates the digestive system, while the lemon provides valuable vitamins, especially vitamin C, and has an alkalizing effect on the body. This morning ritual supports detoxification, helps with hydration after the night, and can also boost metabolism, which aids in maintaining a healthy weight. Drinking lemon water is also an excellent way to support the immune system and improve skin condition, thanks to the lemon's antioxidant properties. This simple habit brings harmony and energy into my life, allowing me to start the day in a healthy and natural way.

PART V

A PRACTICAL PROTECTION STRATEGY

CHAPTER 12

Environmental Contaminants and Food Quality

The modern world faces a significant challenge with environmental contaminants that directly impact the quality of our food. Pollution of air, soil, and water is becoming increasingly common, adversely affecting agricultural crops and livestock. As a result, toxic substances enter the food chain, posing serious health risks to consumers.

Air pollutants, such as particulate matter and heavy metals, settle on plants, affecting their growth and quality. Pesticides, herbicides, and other chemicals used in agriculture penetrate the soil and groundwater, eventually making their way into plants and livestock. Water, which is essential for irrigating crops, can be contaminated with various pollutants, including industrial chemicals.

These contaminants accumulate in the tissues of plants and animals, potentially leading to a range of health issues in humans, such as respiratory diseases, cancers, hormonal imbalances, and neurological problems. Therefore, it is crucial to be aware of the pollutants that can affect our food and take steps to minimize their impact on our health.

In this chapter, we will closely examine different types of environmental pollutants and their effects on food quality. We will also discuss the measures that can be taken by consumers and producers to reduce exposure to these harmful substances and the regulations and practices that can contribute to improving food safety worldwide.

Environmental Contaminants Affecting Food

Environmental contaminants pose a serious threat to the quality of our food. These are various chemical substances that can enter the food chain at different stages of food production—from cultivation, through harvesting, transport, processing, and storage. The most common environmental contaminants affecting food include pesticides, heavy metals, dioxins, PCBs (polychlorinated biphenyls), and microplastics.

Pesticides and Heavy Metals

In previous chapters, we discussed in detail the hazards associated with pesticides and heavy metals such as lead, cadmium, mercury, and arsenic. These contaminants can infiltrate our food from soil and water, leading to serious health issues including hormonal disruptions, neurological disorders, cancers, and fertility problems.

Microplastics

Microplastics are tiny plastic particles less than 5 millimeters in diameter. They can enter food, especially seafood such as fish and shellfish. These small plastic particles primarily come from the breakdown of larger plastic debris in the environment, but also from industrial processes and cosmetic products. In recent years, concerns have grown regarding the potential health impacts of consuming microplastics.

Sources of Microplastics

- **Decomposing Plastic Waste**
  Large pieces of plastic, such as bottles, bags, and packaging, that end up in oceans, lakes, and rivers gradually break down into smaller particles.

- **Cosmetic Products**
  Microplastics are added to many cosmetic products, such as exfoliants and toothpastes, in the form of microbeads. After use, these microbeads enter wastewater systems.

- **Synthetic Clothing**
  Washing synthetic fabrics like polyester releases microplastics, which then enter the water supply and ultimately the environment.

How Do Microplastics Enter Our Food?

- **Seafood:**
  Fish, shellfish, and other marine organisms can inadvertently ingest microplastics present in the water. When these organisms are consumed by humans, microplastics can enter our bodies.

- **Drinking Water:**
  Studies have found microplastics in both bottled and tap water, indicating their presence in our daily diets.

- **Processed Foods:**
  Microplastics can infiltrate food during processing and packaging, especially when the packaging is made from plastic.

Potential Health Effects

- ***Chemical Toxicity***
  Microplastics can contain harmful chemicals such as phthalates, bisphenol A (BPA), and other additives used in plastic production. These substances can leach into the body and cause toxic reactions.

- ***Impact on the Endocrine System***
  Some chemicals present in microplastics can act as endocrine disruptors, interfering with the normal functioning of the hormonal system. This can lead to health issues such as reproductive disorders, thyroid problems, and more.

- ***Inflammation***
  Microplastics can cause inflammation in the body, particularly in the digestive tract. These particles can damage intestinal cells, leading to inflammatory responses and potential digestive problems.

Dioxins and PCBs

Dioxins and polychlorinated biphenyls (PCBs) are groups of chemicals that are by-products of various industrial processes such as waste incineration, chemical manufacturing, and metallurgical processes. They are extremely persistent and can accumulate in the environment, especially in animal fats. Consequently, they can infiltrate food products such as meat, fish, milk, and eggs, posing serious health risks to humans.

Sources of Contamination

- ***Industrial Processes:***
  The burning of industrial waste, production of paper and pulp, oil refining, and other industrial activities can lead to the emission of dioxins and PCBs.

- ***Contaminated Soil and Water:***
  Dioxins and PCBs can leach into soil and groundwater, eventually making their way into crops and aquatic organisms.

- ***Food Chain:***
  These contaminants can accumulate in animal fats, which are then consumed by humans, leading to bioaccumulation in human bodies.

Health Effects

- ***Immune System Damage:***
  Long-term exposure to dioxins and PCBs can weaken the immune system, making the body more susceptible to infections and diseases.

- ***Impact on Fetal Development:***
  Dioxins and PCBs are particularly dangerous for developing fetuses. They can cause neurological development issues, reproductive system problems, and physical development delays.

- ***Increased Cancer Risk:***
  Dioxins and PCBs are classified as carcinogenic substances, increasing the risk of developing various types of cancers, including liver, lung, skin cancers, and lymphoma.

- ***Hormonal Disruptions:***
  These toxic substances can interfere with the endocrine system, leading to hormonal imbalances. They can mimic or block the actions of natural hormones, resulting in fertility problems, menstrual disorders, and thyroid issues.

Strategies for Protecting Against and Avoiding Contaminated Food

In the face of numerous threats related to food contamination, such as pesticides, heavy metals, dioxins, PCBs, and microplastics, adopting a conscious approach to food selection is crucial. Below, we present practical tips for choosing foods with lower contamination risks and discuss the role of organic and bio certifications in this process.

Choosing Products with Lower Contamination Risks

- **Organic Products:**
  Organic products are grown without synthetic pesticides, herbicides, and chemical fertilizers. Choosing certified organic products reduces the risk of exposure to harmful substances.

- **Consuming Local and Seasonal Products:**
  Buying local products from trusted farmers can reduce the risk of contamination. Seasonal products are less likely to contain pesticides, as they are grown in natural conditions without the need for artificial pest control.

- **Thorough Washing and Peeling of Fruits and Vegetables:**
  Washing fruits and vegetables under running water, and in some cases peeling them, can help remove pesticide residues from their

surface. Using natural cleaning agents such as baking soda, apple cider vinegar, or ozonation can be additionally effective.

⇨ **Limiting Consumption of High-Risk Contaminated Products:**
Some products are more prone to contamination, so it's wise to limit their consumption. These include thin-skinned fruits and vegetables (e.g., strawberries, apples), fish from the top of the food chain (e.g., tuna, swordfish), and processed meat products.

The Role of Organic and Bio Certifications

⇨ **Organic Certifications:**
Products labeled with organic certifications, such as EU Organic, USDA Organic, or Bio Suisse, must meet strict standards for cultivation, processing, and packaging. These products are free from synthetic pesticides, GMOs, and limit the use of antibiotics and hormones in animal husbandry.

⇨ **Bio Certifications:**
Bio products are grown sustainably, respecting the environment and animal welfare. Bio certifications ensure that products are free from artificial additives and preservatives, reducing the risk of consuming harmful chemicals.

⇨ **Fair Trade Certifications:**
Although primarily associated with ethical trade standards, Fair Trade certified products often also meet high environmental standards. Purchasing products with this certification supports farmers who use sustainable agricultural practices.

Tips for Making Conscious Food Choices

- ⇨ **Reading Labels:**
  Always check food labels to learn about their ingredients and origin. Avoid products containing artificial additives, preservatives, and other chemicals.

- ⇨ **Buying from Trusted Sources:**
  Choose products from reliable suppliers and farmers who practice sustainable agriculture. Local markets, food cooperatives, and organic food stores are good places to shop.

- ⇨ **Eating a Variety of Foods:**
  A diverse diet can help minimize the risk of exposure to specific contaminants that may be present in high amounts in certain foods.

- ⇨ **Growing Your Own Food:**
  If possible, grow your own fruits and vegetables. This allows you to have complete control over the use of pesticides and soil quality.

Environmental contaminants have a serious impact on the quality of our food and health. Adopting a conscious approach to choosing food products, using water filters, and understanding the benefits of organic certifications can help minimize risks. Let's remember to regularly monitor food quality and choose healthy, sustainable options to protect our health and the future of our planet.

Pesticides, heavy metals, and other chemicals present in the air, water, and soil can infiltrate crops and subsequently enter our bodies through food consumption. High concentrations of these contaminants can lead to numerous health problems, including chronic diseases and metabolic disorders. With growing environmental awareness and concern for health, more and more consumers are seeking ways to effectively clean fruits and vegetables before consumption.

In the next chapter, we will learn how baking soda and apple cider vinegar can help clean fruits and vegetables.

CHAPTER 13

How Baking Soda and Apple Cider Vinegar Can Help Clean Fruits and Vegetables

Homemade methods for cleaning fruits and vegetables are gaining popularity among those concerned about the health and safety of their food. Baking soda and apple cider vinegar are two widely available, inexpensive products that can significantly help remove pesticides and bacteria from the surface of produce.

Effectiveness of Homemade Cleaning Methods

Baking Soda

Baking soda (sodium bicarbonate) neutralizes chemicals and breaks them down into less harmful substances. Studies have shown that washing produce in a baking soda solution for several minutes significantly reduces pesticide residues. A study published in the "Journal of Agricultural and Food Chemistry" found that washing apples in a baking soda solution for 12-15 minutes removes up to 96% of certain pesticides from their surface.

Instructions for Use:

- ⇨ Dissolve 1 tablespoon of baking soda in 2 cups of water.
- ⇨ Soak fruits and vegetables for 5-10 minutes.
- ⇨ Rinse under running water.

Apple Cider Vinegar

Apple cider vinegar contains acetic acid, which acts as a natural antibacterial and antifungal agent. Research shows that apple cider vinegar can effectively remove bacteria such as Escherichia coli and Salmonella from the surface of fruits and vegetables. A study conducted by scientists at the University of Tennessee found that apple cider vinegar can reduce bacterial count by 90%.

Instructions for Use:

- ⇨ Dilute 1 part apple cider vinegar with 3 parts water.
- ⇨ Soak fruits and vegetables for 5-10 minutes.
- ⇨ Rinse under running water.

Combining Baking Soda and Apple Cider Vinegar

The combination of baking soda and apple cider vinegar is often used as a natural cleaning agent for fruits and vegetables. Baking soda acts as an alkalizing agent that helps remove dirt and chemicals from the surface of produce, while apple cider vinegar has antibacterial and antifungal properties that help eliminate microorganisms.

Instructions for Use:

- ⇨ Prepare a solution with 1 tablespoon of baking soda and 1 cup of water.
- ⇨ Soak fruits and vegetables in the baking soda solution for about 5-10 minutes.

- ⇨ Rinse the produce and then soak in a solution of 1 part apple cider vinegar to 3 parts water for another 5-10 minutes.
- ⇨ Rinse thoroughly under running water.

Benefits of Using Natural Methods

- ⇨ **Safety:**
  Non-toxic and safe for health and the environment. Baking soda and apple cider vinegar are natural and non-toxic substances, making them safe for human health and the environment.

- ⇨ **Availability:**
  Easily accessible and affordable. Both ingredients are readily available and inexpensive, making them an attractive alternative to more expensive commercial cleaning agents.

- ⇨ **Effectiveness:**
  Studies confirm they effectively remove pesticides and bacteria. Research has shown that both baking soda and apple cider vinegar are effective in removing pesticides and bacteria from the surface of fruits and vegetables.

Drawbacks of Using Natural Methods

- **Time-Consuming**: The washing process can be more time-consuming.
- **Smell and Taste**: Apple cider vinegar may leave a smell or taste on the produce.

Expert Opinions

Jenny Kingsley*, author of "Cleaning with Baking Soda: The Green and Natural Way to Clean Your Home"*: "This book offers detailed information on various uses of baking soda, including for cleaning fruits and vegetables."

***Emily Thacker**, author of "The Vinegar Book: Vinegar's 1001 Greatest Uses"*: "It covers a wide range of vinegar applications, including cleaning food products, with additional information on its antibacterial properties."

Alternative: Ozonation

For those interested in a quicker method of cleaning fruits and vegetables, ozonation is recommended. This effective disinfection technique rapidly removes contaminants and microorganisms.

In the next chapter, we will discuss food ozonation—a modern method that uses ozone to remove contaminants, bacteria, and viruses from the surface of food products. We will explore how ozonation works, its advantages and disadvantages, and how it can be applied in everyday household practices.

CHAPTER 14

Food Ozonation - A Modern Method of Preservation and Cleaning

In today's world, increasing attention is being given to modern food preservation methods that allow for longer freshness without the need for chemical preservatives. One such innovative technique is ozonation, which is gaining popularity both in households and in the food industry.

Principle and Benefits of Ozonation

How Ozonation Works

Ozonation involves the use of ozone (O3), a gas composed of three oxygen atoms, which has strong oxidizing properties. Ozone can effectively destroy microorganisms such as bacteria, viruses, molds, and fungi that can cause food spoilage. This process occurs through the breakdown of ozone into oxygen and a free oxygen atom, which is highly reactive and interacts with the cell membranes of microorganisms, damaging them and leading to their elimination.

Benefits of Ozonation

- **Extended Freshness:**
  Ozonation significantly extends the shelf life of fresh products such as fruits, vegetables, meat, and fish without the need for chemical preservatives.

- **Food Safety:**
  By eliminating harmful microorganisms, ozonation enhances the safety of consumed products, reducing the risk of food poisoning.

- **Natural Method:**
  Ozone is a natural disinfectant that, after fulfilling its role, decomposes into oxygen, leaving no harmful chemical residues.

- **Reduction of Pesticides:**
  Ozonation can also help reduce pesticide residues on the surface of fruits and vegetables, contributing to a healthier diet.

Practical Applications at Home and in Industry

Ozonation in the Home Kitchen

At home, food ozonation is becoming more accessible thanks to specialized ozone generators that can be easily used in the kitchen and are not a costly investment. Here are some practical applications:

- **Washing Fruits and Vegetables:**
  Immersing fruits and vegetables in ozonated water helps effectively remove pesticides, bacteria, and other contaminants.

- **Storing Meat and Fish:**
  After ozonating meat and fish, they can be placed in airtight

containers to extend their freshness and reduce the risk of bacterial growth.

- ⇨ **Ozonating the Refrigerator:**
  Regularly ozonating the interior of the refrigerator helps keep it clean by eliminating unpleasant odors and bacteria.

Ozonation in the Food Industry

In the food industry, ozonation is widely used at various stages of production and storage:

- ⇨ **Surface Disinfection:**
  Ozonating production lines, conveyor belts, and packaging ensures high hygiene standards and reduces the risk of product contamination.

- ⇨ **Storage and Transport:**
  Warehouses and transportation vehicles equipped with ozonation systems can extend the freshness of large batches of fruits, vegetables, meat, and fish during storage and transport.

- ⇨ **Food Processing:**
  Ozonation can be applied in food processing, such as juice production, where it helps eliminate microorganisms without the need for high temperatures, preserving the natural taste and nutritional value of the products.

How to Ozonate Food at Home

Ozonating food at home is a simple process that can significantly enhance the safety and freshness of the products you consume. Here are the steps to follow:

⇨ **Preparing the Ozone Generator:**
Ensure you have an ozone generator designed for home use. Read the instruction manual to fully understand how the device operates.

⇨ **Preparing the Water Container:**
Fill a large bowl or sink with water. The ozone generator will produce ozone, which dissolves in the water.

⇨ **Adding Food:**
Place fruits, vegetables, meat, eggs, or fish in the water. Make sure all items are fully submerged.

⇨ **Starting the Generator:**
Turn on the ozone generator and let it run for the specified time (usually 10-15 minutes). The ozone will destroy bacteria, viruses, and other contaminants.

⇨ **Rinsing and Drying:**
After the ozonation process is complete, rinse the food with clean water and dry it before storing or cooking.

Safety of Ozonation

Safety for Food

Ozonation is a safe food preservation method because:

- ⇨ **No Chemical Residues:**
  Ozone quickly breaks down into oxygen, leaving no harmful chemical residues on the food.

- ⇨ **Natural Process:**
  It is a natural method that does not alter the taste or nutritional value of the products.

Safety for Users

Ozonation is safe if a few basic guidelines are followed:

- ⇨ **Ventilation:**
  Ensure the room where you use the ozone generator is well-ventilated. High concentrations of ozone can be harmful to the respiratory system.

- ⇨ **Exposure Time:**
  Do not exceed the recommended ozonation time. Prolonged exposure to high concentrations of ozone can be harmful.

- ⇨ **Storage of the Generator:**
  Store the ozone generator in a dry and cool place, away from children.

Ozonation of food is a modern, effective, and safe preservation method that is gaining popularity both in home kitchens and in the food industry.

Thanks to its unique properties, ozone helps extend the freshness of products, improve their safety, and reduce contaminants, contributing to a healthier diet and better well-being.

Short Summary - My Daily Life

Since I purchased a food ozonator, I have been ozonating my groceries. Previously, I used easily accessible and inexpensive baking soda and apple cider vinegar. These methods give me peace of mind, ensuring I am doing everything I can to protect my body from harmful substances. The entire process is not labor-intensive, as I do it while cooking dinner, preparing breakfast, or during any free time spent in the kitchen.

It's just an additional task during daily meal preparation, and a bit of organization is all it takes. Sometimes, after larger shopping trips, I clean products in batches, preserving their freshness for longer. Meanwhile, I perform other household chores because during the ozonation process, I don't have to do anything – just place the products in water, turn on the ozonator, and after 15 minutes, rinse with water and set aside to dry.

Since I eat most meals at home, I am reassured about the amount of harmful substances I consume, even when eating out. It's a small change but very important. Adopting and incorporating this habit into daily life significantly eases the burden on our bodies.

PART VI

DIET AND HEALTH

CHAPTER 15

Bio, Eco, Organic – Marketing or Real Value?

Nowadays, more and more people pay attention to food labels, seeking healthy and safe dietary options. The terms "bio," "eco," and "organic" have become synonymous with a healthy lifestyle. But is this just a clever marketing ploy, or is there real value that translates to our health?

The Importance of Certifications and Regulations

Products labeled as "bio," "eco," or "organic" must meet specific standards regulated by appropriate institutions. In the European Union, organic products must be grown without synthetic pesticides, herbicides, and artificial fertilizers. Additionally, the use of GMOs (genetically modified organisms) is prohibited in their production. These regulations aim to ensure that such products are not only safe for consumers but also more environmentally friendly.

Health Benefits of Organic Products

Studies show that organic products may contain higher concentrations of certain nutrients, such as vitamins, minerals, and antioxidants. For example, organic fruits and vegetables often have higher levels of vitamin C, iron, magnesium, and phosphorus. Additionally, these products typically contain fewer pesticides and other harmful chemicals, which can have a positive impact on our health.

Impact on the Environment

Organic farming is often more sustainable than conventional farming methods. Practices such as crop rotation, the use of natural fertilizers, and the protection of biodiversity help maintain soil health and ecosystems. Additionally, limiting the use of pesticides and herbicides reduces groundwater and surface water pollution, which is beneficial for the entire natural environment.

Costs and Availability

One of the main challenges associated with organic products is their higher price compared to conventional products. Higher costs stem from more labor-intensive farming methods and smaller yields. However, increasing consumer awareness and growing demand for organic products are leading to greater availability and competitive prices.

Is It Worth Investing in Organic Food?

The decision to choose organic products depends on individual priorities and budget. For me, as well as for many others, avoiding pesticides and chemicals and supporting sustainable farming practices is crucial. It's also important to note the taste and quality of the products – the difference is noticeable. Ultimately, choosing organic food can contribute to better health and environmental protection, making it a valuable investment.

Short Summary - My Daily Life

On a daily basis, my shopping basket includes the types of products mentioned above. Choosing bio, eco, and organic products is not only a matter of health but also ethics and environmental responsibility. While higher costs can be a barrier, the health and environmental benefits make it worth considering their inclusion in a daily diet. Sometimes it's better to eat less but consume nutrient-rich foods than to fill our bodies with nutritionally poor products loaded with pesticides, heavy metals, and other toxins that wreak havoc on our health.

Unhealthy snacks like chips, ice cream, cookies, alcohol, and similar products clutter our bodies and drain our budgets, often without us realizing it. It's worth giving them up and investing that money in high-quality, nutrient-rich foods. Nutritious foods nourish our bodies, so we eat less and don't feel hungry. Our bodies will thank us, and we will enjoy good health and well-being.

Next, we will discuss the impact of diet on physical and mental health, considering how our daily food choices can affect our mood, energy levels, and overall well-being.

CHAPTER 16

Food and Lifestyle Diseases: How Our Choices Shape Health

In today's world, our dietary choices have a profound impact on health. With technological advancements and lifestyle changes, there has been a noticeable increase in lifestyle diseases such as obesity, type 2 diabetes, cardiovascular diseases, cancers, joint problems, vision issues, women's health problems, and skin conditions.

Looking back to the 1970s, the physiques of men and women were significantly different. Obesity was a marginal issue, whereas today it is a global problem. Times and food have changed. Understanding how diet affects our health is key to preventing these ailments and improving quality of life.

Many scientific studies indicate that poor diet can significantly influence the development and progression of various diseases. Unhealthy eating habits, such as excessive intake of trans fats, saturated fats, sugar, and processed foods, can lead to serious conditions, including cardiovascular diseases, type 2 diabetes, obesity, cancers, and mental health disorders. Being aware of these risks and making informed dietary decisions is crucial for maintaining health and well-being.

Below are a few tips on healthy and unhealthy products for selected health conditions as a guide. It's worth delving deeper into the topic to better understand how our food choices affect health.

Obesity and Overweight

Obesity is one of the most serious epidemics of our time, affecting millions of people worldwide. A high-calorie diet rich in processed foods, sugars, and saturated fats is the primary cause of overweight and obesity. Excessive body weight increases the risk of many serious diseases, including type 2 diabetes, heart diseases, and certain cancers.

Products That Increase the Risk of Obesity

- **White Bread and Fast Food**: Wheat bread, rolls, sugary cereals, hamburgers, fries, pizza.
- **Sweets**: Cookies, candy bars, sugary drinks.
- **Snacks**: Chips, pretzels, crackers.
- **Carbonated and Sugary Drinks**: Cola, sodas, 100% juices.

Products That Support Health

- ✓ **Colorful Vegetables and Fruits**: With a focus on green vegetables and dark-colored fruits such as blueberries, raspberries, cherries.
- ✓ **Whole Grain Products**: Oatmeal, whole grain bread, graham bread, coarse grains, whole grain pasta.
- ✓ **Good Sources of Protein**: Poultry, fish, eggs, legumes, and nuts.

Making healthier food choices can significantly impact weight management and overall health. By prioritizing nutrient-dense foods and minimizing the intake of processed and high-calorie products, individuals can reduce their risk of obesity and related diseases.

Type 2 Diabetes

Type 2 diabetes is closely linked to diet and lifestyle. Consuming large amounts of simple sugars and processed foods can lead to insulin resistance, which can eventually result in diabetes. Prolonged high blood sugar levels can cause serious health complications such as kidney damage, heart problems, and nerve damage.

Products That Increase the Risk of Diabetes

- **Sugary Drinks**: Cola, fruit juices with added sugar.
- **White Bread and White Flour Products**: Bread, pasta, cakes.
- **Sweets and Desserts**: Cakes, cookies, candy bars, sweetened yogurts.
- **Processed Foods and Saturated Fats**: Fast food, deli meats (bacon, sausage), fatty fried meats.
- **Alcohol**.

Products That Support Health

- ✓ **Vegetables**: Zucchini, raw carrots, celery, cauliflower, cucumbers, broccoli, cabbage.
- ✓ **Fruits**: Apples, berries, kiwi, plums.
- ✓ **Good Sources of Protein**: Eggs, lean poultry, lean beef, fish.
- ✓ **Legumes**: Lentils, beans, chickpeas.
- ✓ **Whole Grain Products**: Low glycemic index products such as whole grain bread, brown rice, bulgur, barley, or pearl barley.
- ✓ **Healthy Fats**: Avocado, olive oil, nuts.

Adopting a diet rich in vegetables, fruits, lean proteins, legumes, whole grains, and healthy fats can help manage and prevent type 2 diabetes.

Avoiding processed foods, sugary drinks, and high-calorie snacks is crucial for maintaining stable blood sugar levels and overall health.

Cardiovascular Diseases

Heart and blood vessel diseases are the leading cause of death worldwide. A diet high in saturated and trans fats, salt, and processed foods can lead to high cholesterol, hypertension, and atherosclerosis, which in turn increases the risk of heart attack and stroke.

Products That Increase the Risk of Cardiovascular Diseases

- **Fatty Meats and Deli Meats**: Bacon, sausage, pork knuckle, kabanos, ham.
- **Fried Foods**: Meat, fish fried in deep fat.
- **Fast Food**: Pizza, fries, hamburgers, chips, etc.

Products That Support Health

- ✓ **Healthy Fats**: Olive oil, avocado, nuts.
- ✓ **Lean Proteins**: Fish, poultry, legumes, eggs.
- ✓ **Vegetables and Fruits**: Rich in fiber and antioxidants: green vegetables and dark fruits.

Eating a diet rich in healthy fats, lean proteins, and a variety of vegetables and fruits can help reduce the risk of cardiovascular diseases. Avoiding fatty meats, fried foods, and fast food is crucial for maintaining heart health and overall well-being.

Cancers

Some studies suggest that diet can influence the risk of developing cancer. Consuming large amounts of poor-quality red meat, sugar, and processed foods may increase the risk of colorectal cancer. Conversely, a diet rich in fruits, vegetables, and fiber may have protective effects.

Products That Increase the Risk of Cancers:

- **Simple Sugars and Sweets**: Cookies, cakes, ice cream, candy bars, milk chocolate.
- **Red Meat and Processed Meats**: Hams, bacon (pork products), kabanos.
- **Food High in Preservatives and Artificial Additives**: Sweets, colored drinks, hams, ready-to-eat fast food products.
- **Alcohol and Stimulants**: Excessive consumption of beer, wine, and other alcoholic beverages, as well as tobacco use.

Products That Support Health:

- ✓ **Low-Starch Vegetables**: Lettuce, cucumber, tomatoes, cabbage, broccoli, cauliflower, kale, kohlrabi, sauerkraut, Swiss chard, bell pepper, turnip, asparagus, spinach, chicory, celery, onion, garlic, parsley, radish, leek.
- ✓ **Fruits**: Apples, blackberries, blueberries, raspberries, cherries, pomegranate, cranberries, citrus fruits, grapes, papaya, goji berries.
- ✓ **Minimally Refined and Processed Grains**: Whole grain bread, coarse grains, brown rice, bran, natural cereal flakes.
- ✓ **Natural Antioxidants**: Garlic, turmeric, ginger.

- ✓ **Legumes**: Sources of fiber and protein: peas, beans, lentils, broad beans, chickpeas.

Adopting a diet rich in low-starch vegetables, fruits, whole grains, natural antioxidants, and legumes can help reduce the risk of cancer. Avoiding high-sugar, red meat, processed foods, and excessive alcohol consumption is crucial for minimizing cancer risk and promoting overall health.

Joint Problems

Diet can also affect joint health. Consuming excess saturated fats and processed foods can lead to inflammation, worsening joint conditions.

Products That Increase the Risk of Joint Problems

- **Fast Food and Processed Meats**: Ready-made frozen meals, fatty meats, hams, and other processed meats.
- **Simple Sugars and Sweets**: Candies, sugary drinks, highly processed foods, ice cream, cakes, breakfast cereals, desserts, and fruit-flavored yogurts.
- **Foods High in Trans Fats**: Primarily found in chips, fast food, pretzels, margarines, cookies, ready-made products (e.g., powdered soups and sauces), and pre-cooked dishes.

Products That Support Joint Health

- ✓ **Fatty Fish**: Rich in omega-3 fatty acids, which have anti-inflammatory effects. The highest levels of omega-3 fatty acids are found in marine fish such as salmon, herring, rainbow trout, and mackerel. Due to contamination, Baltic fish and tuna are not recommended.

- ✓ **Leafy Vegetables**: Rich in vitamins and minerals, especially vitamin C, which supports collagen production important for joint health: fresh bell peppers, black currants, rose hips, citrus fruits, Brussels sprouts, broccoli, sauerkraut, parsley.
- ✓ **Nuts and Seeds**: Rich in monounsaturated fatty acids that have anti-inflammatory effects, as well as being good sources of protein and fiber, such as almonds, walnuts, pine nuts, pistachios, and flaxseeds.
- ✓ **Collagen-Rich Products**: Gelatin (jellies, fish in aspic, pork and veal trotters), chicken feet.

Adopting a diet that includes omega-3 fatty acids, leafy vegetables, nuts, seeds, and collagen-rich foods can help support joint health and reduce inflammation. Avoiding fast food, processed meats, sugary foods, and trans fats is crucial for maintaining healthy joints and reducing the risk of joint problems.

Vision Problems

Diet can affect eye health and the risk of eye diseases such as macular degeneration.

Products That Increase the Risk of Vision Problems

- **Processed Foods**: Fast food and fried and processed meats like sausages, bacon.
- **Sugary Drinks, Sugars, and Sweets**: Juices, cola, and other colored drinks, cakes, cookies, candy bars, fruit-flavored yogurts.
- **Trans Fats**: Chips, fried foods like bacon.

Products That Support Eye Health

- ✓ **Carrots and Other Beta-Carotene Rich Vegetables**: Dried apricots, kale, fresh apricots, parsley, melon, spinach, dried plums, peaches, sorrel, chives, pumpkin, orange, broccoli.
- ✓ **Fruits and Vegetables Rich in Lutein and Zeaxanthin**: Lutein is found in green vegetables like lettuce, parsley, broccoli, spinach, and kale. Zeaxanthin sources include green peas, corn, and zucchinis. The highest amounts of anthocyanins are in blueberries and blackberries.
- ✓ **Fish Rich in Omega-3 Fatty Acids**: The highest levels of omega-3 fatty acids are found in marine fish such as salmon, herring, rainbow trout, and mackerel. Due to contamination, Baltic fish and tuna are not recommended.
- ✓ **Dairy Products**: Eggs, egg yolks, high-quality meat.
- ✓ **Seeds and Nuts**: Pumpkin seeds, sunflower seeds, flaxseeds, hazelnuts, walnuts, Brazil nuts.

Incorporating beta-carotene-rich vegetables, lutein and zeaxanthin-rich fruits and vegetables, omega-3-rich fish, dairy, seeds, and nuts into your diet can help maintain eye health and reduce the risk of vision problems. Avoiding processed foods, sugary drinks, sweets, and trans fats is essential for preserving eye health and preventing eye diseases.

Women's Health Issues

Women's health issues, such as thyroid disorders, premenstrual syndrome (PMS), and fertility problems, can also be linked to diet.

Products That Increase the Risk of Women's Health Issues:

- **Processed Foods**: Fast food, candy bars, chips.
- **Simple Sugars and Sweets**: Candy bars, muesli, granola, milk chocolates.
- **Alcoholic Beverages**: Wine, liqueurs, whisky, and others.
- **Wheat and Dairy Products**: Cheese, milk, white bread; gluten and dairy products (casein).

Products That Support Women's Health:

A diet should be based on healthy fats, valuable proteins, and antioxidants.

- ✓ **Low Progesterone**: Cruciferous vegetables, purple fruits, legumes, nuts.
- ✓ **High Estrogen**: Bitter vegetables (horseradish, mustard, chicory, artichoke), buckwheat, turmeric, apples, grapes.
- ✓ **Low Estrogen**: Eggs, offal, yeast, legumes, nuts, pomegranate, flax, rhubarb.
- ✓ **High Testosterone**: Marine fish, vegetable oils, cinnamon, white mulberry, seeds, nuts, grains.
- ✓ **Low Testosterone**: Spelt, oats, mushrooms, vegetable oils, cruciferous vegetables, seaweed, pumpkin seeds, high-quality meat, seafood.
- ✓ **Hypothyroidism**: Marine fish, algae, seafood, black cumin, quinoa, oats, spelt, amaranth, red and purple fruits, onion vegetables, turnips, squash, eggs.
- ✓ **High Cortisol**: Green tea, cocoa, broccoli, sea buckthorn, rosehip, purple fruits, seeds, nuts, avocado.
- ✓ **Low Cortisol**: Vegetable oils, sprouts, citrus fruits, turmeric, ginger, sesame, almonds, marine fish, eggs, legumes.

Incorporating these foods into the diet can help manage specific women's health issues by balancing hormones and providing essential nutrients. Avoiding processed foods, simple sugars, alcohol, and certain wheat and dairy products can further support overall health and well-being.

Skin Problems

Diet has a significant impact on skin health. Consuming large amounts of processed foods, sugars, and trans fats can lead to skin problems such as acne, eczema, and premature aging.

Products That Increase the Risk of Skin Problems:

- **Simple Sugars and Sweets**: Cakes, candy bars, milk chocolates.
- **Fast Food and Processed Foods**: Chips, pretzels, pizza, ready-made frozen meals.
- **Products Containing Gluten and Casein**: Wheat bread, cakes, pasta, dairy products.
- **Colored Carbonated Drinks**: Juices, energy drinks, cola.
- **Nuts**: Pine nuts, peanuts, peanut butter.
- **Protein**: Soy and chicken egg protein.

Products That Support Skin Health:

- ✓ **Omega-3 and Omega-6 Fatty Acids**: Fatty marine fish (e.g., salmon, mackerel), walnuts, hazelnuts, sunflower and pumpkin seeds, olive oil, black cumin oil, avocado, and flaxseed.
- ✓ **Fruits and Vegetables**: Especially green leafy vegetables and berries, as well as spices (e.g., ginger, turmeric).
- ✓ **Whole Grain Products**: Grains and rice, including amaranth and quinoa.

- ✓ **Legumes**: Beans, peas, chickpeas, and lentils, which are rich sources of plant protein, fiber, and minerals.
- ✓ **Water**: Helps maintain skin hydration.

Incorporating omega-3 and omega-6 fatty acids, a variety of fruits and vegetables, whole grains, legumes, and sufficient water intake into your diet can help improve and maintain skin health. Avoiding processed foods, simple sugars, and certain nuts and proteins is crucial for reducing the risk of skin problems.

Short Summary - My Daily Life

We must realize that we are what we eat. Our bodies need nourishment from foods rich in vitamins, minerals, and micro- and macroelements. All diseases and dysfunctions of our bodies signal that we are doing something wrong.

From my own experience, I can say that I healed myself through diet. I no longer indulge in junk food but nourish my body. Before starting my healthy eating journey, I "fought" with various diets, trying to be satisfied with my body, not knowing that the problem lay in intolerances and the body's burdens. Since childhood, I struggled with allergies, swelling, and the beginnings of asthma. I thought diets would change something, but bad moods, digestive problems, and swelling, the so-called yo-yo effect, always returned when I went back to my old eating habits. After changing my lifestyle and eating habits, all my ailments gave way to well-being.

Our daily food choices have a huge impact on health and quality of life. Avoiding processed foods and products rich in sugars and saturated fats can help prevent many lifestyle diseases. A healthy, balanced diet rich in natural products is the key to a long and healthy life.

CHAPTER 17

Poor Food Quality – Vitamin and Mineral Deficiencies – How It Affects Our Mind and Body

The modern diet is often high in calories but low in essential vitamins and minerals. Poor food quality leads to deficiencies that can have serious consequences for our physical and mental health. In this chapter, we will discuss how the lack of key nutrients affects our mind and body and ways to improve the quality of our diet.

Importance of Vitamins and Minerals

Vitamins and minerals are essential for the proper functioning of the body. They play a key role in many biochemical processes, including energy production, immune system function, DNA synthesis, and the health of the skin, bones, and muscles. Deficiencies in these nutrients can lead to numerous health problems.

Impact of Deficiencies on Physical Health

- ***Weakened Immune System:***
  Deficiencies in vitamins A, C, and E, as well as minerals like zinc

and selenium, weaken the immune system, increasing susceptibility to infections, slowing wound healing, and raising the risk of chronic inflammation.

- ***Bone and Muscle Problems:***
  A deficiency in vitamin D and calcium leads to weakened bones, which can result in osteoporosis and an increased risk of fractures. Lack of magnesium, potassium, and vitamin B1 (thiamine) affects muscle function, leading to cramps, weakness, and fatigue.

- ***Cardiovascular Diseases:***
  Deficiencies in B vitamins, especially B6, B12, and folic acid, can lead to elevated homocysteine levels in the blood, a risk factor for cardiovascular diseases. Lack of potassium and magnesium also negatively impacts blood pressure and heart health.

- ***Skin Problems:***
  Vitamin A deficiency can cause dry skin and vision problems, while lack of biotin and zinc can lead to hair loss, brittle nails, and other dermatological issues.

- ***Hematopoietic Disorders:***
  Deficiency in iron, vitamin B12, and folic acid can lead to anemia, manifested by weakness, fatigue, headaches, and pale skin.

- ***Digestive Issues:***
  Lack of vitamin B1 (thiamine) can lead to digestive disturbances, appetite loss, and impaired intestinal function, while insufficient fiber intake can cause constipation and other digestive problems.

Impact of Deficiencies on Mental Health

➤ ***Depression and Anxiety:***
Deficiencies in vitamin D, B6, B12, and folic acid are associated with a higher risk of depression and anxiety disorders. These vitamins are essential for the production of neurotransmitters such as serotonin and dopamine, which regulate mood.

➤ ***Memory and Concentration Problems:***
Deficiencies in vitamin B12, folic acid, iron, and iodine can lead to memory problems, concentration issues, and overall cognitive dysfunction. These nutrients are crucial for brain health and neurological functions.

➤ ***Fatigue and Lack of Energy:***
Deficiencies in iron, vitamin B12, and folic acid can lead to anemia, which manifests as chronic fatigue, weakness, and lack of energy. These nutrients are essential for the production of red blood cells and the transport of oxygen throughout the body.

How to Improve Diet Quality

⇨ **Eating a Variety of Foods:**
Introducing a variety of food sources into the diet, such as vegetables, fruits, whole grains, lean proteins, and healthy fats, ensures an adequate intake of vitamins and minerals.

⇨ **Choosing Natural and Unprocessed Foods:**
Avoiding processed foods, which are often low in nutrients and high in empty calories, can significantly improve diet quality. Instead, opt for fresh, natural products.

⇨ **Supplementation:**
In some cases, especially when access to fresh produce is limited, vitamin and mineral supplementation is necessary. However, it's important to consult with a doctor or a qualified professional before starting supplementation to avoid excessive intake of certain nutrients.

Short Summary - My Daily Life

Being aware of how nutrient deficiencies affect our bodies, I regularly monitor and replenish them through diet or supplementation. Issues like fatigue, concentration problems, hair loss, and brittle nails have disappeared.

Vitamin and mineral deficiencies caused by poor food quality have serious consequences for our physical and mental health. By maintaining a varied and high-quality diet and considering supplementation, we can prevent many health problems and improve our well-being. In the following chapters, we will explore more detailed strategies and examples to help implement positive changes in daily nutrition.

PART VII

CONSCIOUS CHOICES

CHAPTER 18

The Role of Healthy Fats in the Body

In today's world, where healthy eating is becoming increasingly popular, the role of fats in the diet often sparks much controversy. In this chapter, we will examine how healthy fats affect our bodies, what their sources are, and why they are essential for maintaining good health.

Importance of Fats for Health

Fats are one of the essential macronutrients necessary for the proper functioning of the body. They play a crucial role in many biochemical processes, including hormone production, the absorption of fat-soluble vitamins (A, D, E, K), and the construction of cell membranes.

Types of Healthy Fats

Unsaturated Fats

- ✓ **Monounsaturated Fats:**
  Found in olive oil, avocados, and nuts. They help lower bad cholesterol (LDL) and raise good cholesterol (HDL).

✓ **Polyunsaturated Fats:**
Found in fish, flaxseeds, and plant oils. These fats are important for brain function and vision.

✓ **Omega-3 and Omega-6 Fatty Acids:**
Omega-3 Fatty Acids,present in fish, flaxseeds, and walnuts, these fats have anti-inflammatory properties and support heart and brain health. Omega-6 Fatty Acids, found in plant oils and seeds, these fats are also important but should be consumed in the right proportion to Omega-3s for optimal health.

Health Benefits

⇨ **Heart Health:**
Healthy fats help lower LDL cholesterol levels, reducing the risk of cardiovascular diseases. Omega-3 fatty acids can also lower blood pressure and reduce the risk of arrhythmias. Studies show that a diet rich in Omega-3s decreases the risk of heart attack and stroke.

⇨ **Brain Function and Mental Health:**
Fats, especially Omega-3s, are crucial for brain health. They support neuron development, improve memory and concentration, and may reduce the risk of depression and anxiety disorders. Research suggests that Omega-3 supplementation can improve symptoms of depression and ADHD.

⇨ **Vitamin Absorption:**
Fats are essential for the absorption of vitamins A, D, E, and K. Without adequate fats in the diet, the body may struggle to absorb these vital nutrients.

Sources of Healthy Fats

✓ **Olive Oil:**
Rich in monounsaturated fats, excellent for salads and cooking.

✓ **Avocado:**
Contains monounsaturated fats as well as vitamins and minerals.

✓ **Fatty Fish:**
Salmon, mackerel, and sardines are high in Omega-3 fatty acids.

✓ **Nuts and Seeds:**
Almonds, walnuts, and flaxseeds provide healthy fats and protein.

✓ **Plant Oils:**
Pumpkin seed oil and flaxseed oil are good sources of polyunsaturated fats.

How to Incorporate Healthy Fats into Your Diet

⇨ **Meal Planning:**
Include healthy fats in your daily meals by adding olive oil to salads, avocado to sandwiches, and nuts as snacks.

⇨ **Cooking:**
Avoid excessive heat when cooking with oils to preserve their health benefits.

⇨ **Supplementation:**
If you find it difficult to get enough healthy fats from your diet, consider supplementation, especially Omega-3s, after consulting with a doctor or a qualified professional.

Scientific Studies Confirming the Benefits of Healthy Fats

Scientific research provides ample evidence of the health benefits associated with consuming healthy fats. Here are a few key studies:

Heart Health

Studies have shown that a diet rich in Omega-3 fatty acids can reduce the risk of cardiovascular diseases. For example, a study published in the *Journal of the American College of Cardiology* found that regular consumption of fish high in Omega-3s significantly lowers the risk of heart attack and stroke.

Brain Function and Mental Health

Omega-3 supplementation can improve symptoms of depression and ADHD. A study conducted by the National Institutes of Health indicated that children with ADHD who took Omega-3 supplements showed improvements in concentration and cognitive functions.

Vitamin Absorption

Fats are essential for the absorption of fat-soluble vitamins. Research shows that consuming healthy fats with meals rich in vitamins A, D, E, and K improves their bioavailability and effectiveness in the body.

Short Summary - My Daily Life

In my diet, fats play a crucial role. As mentioned before, my kitchen includes various types of fats, both plant-based and animal-based. Fats are essential for the proper functioning of our body, nourishing our hormonal, cardiovascular, digestive systems, and brain function.

We often fear fats due to the concern of gaining weight, but the real culprits are junk food, sugar-rich diets, excess carbohydrates, and trans fats. Good fats are calorie-dense, making us eat less but with higher nutritional value. We don't need a large quantity of food, just valuable nutrients. Remember this and incorporate good fats into our meals so our bodies can function optimally and enjoy good health.

Now it's time to delve into another important topic that will help us make more informed dietary choices – reading labels. Understanding the information on food labels is key to healthy eating and avoiding harmful ingredients.

CHAPTER 19

Reading Labels - The Key to Informed Food Choices

When dietary choices have a direct impact on our health, the ability to read food labels is essential. Labels provide valuable information that can help us make informed and healthy choices. In this chapter, we will look at how to correctly interpret labels and what to pay attention to, so our dietary choices are the best they can be.

Why Reading Labels is Important

Food labels contain information that helps us understand exactly what we are eating. Knowing this information allows us to avoid harmful ingredients such as excess sugar, salt, or trans fats, identify allergens, compare products for their nutritional value, and make choices that support our health goals.

Key Elements of Labels

Nutritional Values

The nutritional values table is one of the most important elements of a label. It contains information about calories and the content of macronutrients such as proteins, fats, and carbohydrates. It's also important to pay attention to:

⇨ **Fiber:**
High fiber content supports digestion.

⇨ **Sugars:**
Avoid products with high amounts of added sugars.

⇨ **Fats:**
Check if saturated and trans fats are at low levels.

⇨ **Ingredient List:**
The ingredient list names all the ingredients in the product in descending order by weight. The shorter and more understandable the list, the better. Avoid products with long ingredient lists, especially if they contain many chemicals or preservatives.

⇨ **Allergens:**
Labels must list allergens such as nuts, gluten, lactose, or soy. This is particularly important for people with allergies or food intolerances.

⇨ **Serving Information:**
Pay attention to serving information, as calories and nutrient content are usually given per serving, not for the entire product. Check how many servings the package contains to avoid consuming more calories and nutrients than you intended.

By focusing on these key elements, you can make healthier and more informed choices that align with your dietary needs and health goals.

Harmfulness of E Additives

What are E Additives?

E additives are substances added to food to enhance its taste, appearance, shelf life, or texture. Each E additive has a unique number used on food product labels.

Harmful E Additives

Some E additives can have negative effects on health, especially with long-term consumption. Here are a few examples:

- **E102 (Tartrazine):**
  This is a synthetic yellow dye that can cause allergic reactions, hyperactivity in children, and other intolerance symptoms. Tartrazine is commonly used in beverages, sweets, and processed foods.

- **E220 (Sulfur Dioxide):**
  Used as a preservative in dried fruits, wines, and processed meats. It can cause asthma reactions, respiratory irritations, and other health problems in sensitive individuals.

- **E621 (Monosodium Glutamate):**
  A flavor enhancer commonly used in processed foods, sauces, and instant soups. It can cause headaches, nausea, dizziness, and other intolerance reactions known as "Chinese restaurant syndrome."

- **E951 (Aspartame):**
  An artificial sweetener used in diet drinks and low-calorie products. There are controversies regarding its safety, with some studies suggesting potential risks to the nervous system.

- **E123 (Amaranth):**
  A red dye banned in some countries due to its potential carcinogenic effects. It can also cause allergic reactions and intolerances.

How to Avoid Harmful Additives

Always check the ingredient list and avoid products containing harmful E additives. Choose natural products without chemical additives, and try to prepare meals at home using fresh ingredients.

⇨ **Compare Products:**
Compare products based on their nutritional values per 100 grams or per serving. Check the content of sugars, fats, salt, and fiber to choose the healthier option.

⇨ **Avoid Marketing Gimmicks:**
Don't be misled by labels advertising the product as "natural" or "fat-free." Focus on the nutritional values table and the ingredient list to accurately assess whether the product is genuinely healthy.

⇨ **Watch for Hidden Sugars:**
Sugar can be hidden under many names, such as high-fructose corn syrup, sucrose, dextrose, or molasses. Carefully read the ingredient list to avoid excessive added sugars.

Studies Confirming the Benefits of Consciously Reading Labels

Research indicates that people who regularly read labels tend to eat healthier and maintain a healthier body weight. For example, a study published in the *Journal of the Academy of Nutrition and Dietetics* found that individuals who read food labels consume fewer calories and saturated fats compared to those who do not.

Short Summary - My Daily Life

The ability to read food labels is crucial for making informed dietary choices. I've developed this habit, and I read labels during every shopping trip. Often, products labeled as healthy, gluten-free, or casein-free are high in simple sugars and unhealthy fats. This is a trap we must watch out for. Juices and snacks can contain surprisingly large amounts of sugars, not to mention fast food.

It's worth taking some time while shopping to look at product labels and their ingredients. Sometimes, the list of harmful ingredients is overwhelming, and we may not realize what we are consuming.

By understanding the information on labels, we can avoid harmful ingredients, identify allergens, and make choices that support our health goals. Remember, the shorter the ingredient list, the better. Food should be simple and nutritious, not filled with E additives that harm us.

Now, let's move on to the next chapter, where we will explore the myths and truths about superfoods. Are they really as wonderful as they are portrayed?

CHAPTER 20

Superfoods - Myths and Truths

In recent years, the concept of "superfoods" has become extremely popular. These products are advertised as having exceptional health benefits, often surpassing those of traditional foods. In this chapter, we will explore what superfoods really are, the myths surrounding them, and the actual health benefits associated with their consumption.

What Are Superfoods?

Superfoods is a term used to describe foods that are particularly rich in nutrients such as vitamins, minerals, antioxidants, and other bioactive compounds. Some of the most commonly mentioned superfoods include goji berries, chia seeds, spirulina, acai, quinoa, and many others.

Myths and Facts about Superfoods

It is often said that superfoods are just a marketing gimmick with no real impact on health. While they are indeed promoted in a way that can raise doubts, many of these products have scientifically proven health benefits. Superfoods can be a valuable addition to the diet, providing nutrient-rich ingredients that support health and well-being.

Actual Health Benefits of Superfoods

Superfoods can indeed offer numerous health benefits. Here are a few examples:

- ✓ **Goji Berries:**
  Rich in vitamin C, antioxidants, and carotenoids. They can support the immune system and improve eye health.

- ✓ **Chia Seeds:**
  A source of Omega-3 fatty acids, fiber, and protein. They support heart health and the digestive system.

- ✓ **Spirulina:**
  High in protein, B vitamins, and antioxidants. It can support immune health and detoxification. It's important to source it from a reputable supplier.

- ✓ **Cacao:**
  Cacao beans contain magnesium, iron, phosphorus, zinc, theobromine, caffeine, polyphenols, tryptophan, vitamins A, C, E, and B vitamins. This wide range of substances has beneficial effects on the human body.

- ✓ **Acai:**
  Contains high levels of antioxidants, especially polyphenols. It can support heart health and has anti-inflammatory properties.

- ✓ **Quinoa:**
  A complete protein containing all essential amino acids, rich in fiber and minerals such as magnesium and iron. It supports cardiovascular health and helps maintain a healthy weight.

- ✓ **Moringa:**
  Moringa leaves are rich in vitamins A, C, E, and minerals like calcium and potassium. Moringa has anti-inflammatory and antioxidant properties that can support skin health and the immune system.

- ✓ **Turmeric:**
  Contains curcumin, which has strong anti-inflammatory and antioxidant properties. It can support joint and digestive health and reduce the risk of cardiovascular diseases.

- ✓ **Matcha:**
  Matcha green tea is rich in catechins, particularly EGCG, which have strong antioxidant properties. Matcha can support brain health, improve concentration, and help maintain a healthy weight.

- ✓ **Flaxseed:**
  It is an excellent source of fiber (both soluble and insoluble), minerals such as calcium, magnesium, and phosphorus, vitamins A, C, F, and E, as well as plant-based protein.

- ✓ **Barley Grass Juice:**
  Powdered barley grass juice boosts immunity and prevents inflammation. It is rich in chlorophyll, vitamins, minerals, amino acids, carotenoids, enzymes, and antioxidants. This superfood supports cell construction and regeneration, serving as a natural source of growth hormone that aids in self-healing.

- ✓ **Bee Bread:**
  Bee bread is rich in nutrients that support health on multiple

levels. It contains proteins and essential amino acids, crucial for tissue building and regeneration, along with B vitamins that support the nervous system and metabolism. Bee bread also includes antioxidants such as vitamins C, E, and A, which protect cells from oxidative damage while boosting the immune system. Additionally, it provides essential minerals like iron and magnesium, which help maintain healthy bones and muscles, and it has prebiotic properties that promote the growth of beneficial gut bacteria.

How to Incorporate Superfoods into Your Diet

Incorporating superfoods into your diet can be simple and delicious. Here are a few tips:

- ⇨ Add chia seeds and cacao to smoothies, yogurt, or oatmeal.
- ⇨ Use spirulina as an addition to juices or smoothies.
- ⇨ Introduce quinoa as a substitute for rice or pasta in salads and main dishes.
- ⇨ Eat goji berries as a snack or add them to muesli.
- ⇨ Add matcha powder to smoothies, yogurt, or baked goods.
- ⇨ Include turmeric in dishes such as curries, soups, or sauces.
- ⇨ Add moringa leaves to salads, smoothies, or juices.

Scientific Research on Superfoods

More and more scientific studies are examining the health benefits of superfoods. For example, research published in the *Journal of Agricultural and Food Chemistry* found that acai berries have high antioxidant content, which can protect cells from oxidative damage.

Short Summary - My Daily Life

Superfoods can be a valuable addition to a healthy diet, offering numerous health benefits due to their high nutrient content. However, the key to good health is a varied, balanced diet rich in diverse foods. It is important that superfoods are of good quality and free from harmful substances. In my kitchen, I include all the mentioned superfoods, adding them to various dishes, salads, smoothies, and desserts, and also enjoying them as snacks.

Superfoods are a valuable addition, offering a wealth of nutrients, but they are not the only way to enhance our diet. There are many other strategies we can use to support our health. One of the next topics is functional foods. In the next chapter, we will explore when and which products to choose to provide real health benefits.

CHAPTER 21

Functional Foods – What You Need to Know

In today's fast-paced world, where daily responsibilities can make it challenging to maintain a balanced diet, functional foods are becoming increasingly popular. However, it's important to understand when and which products to choose to truly reap health benefits.

What is Functional Food?

Functional food refers to products that not only provide basic nutrients such as proteins, fats, carbohydrates, vitamins, and minerals but also offer additional health benefits. These products can support health in more direct and specific ways than regular foods. Functional foods can include natural products like nuts and berries, as well as fortified foods such as probiotic yogurts, vitamin-enriched juices, and foods containing bioactive compounds.

Types of Functional Foods

Natural Functional Foods

- ✓ **Nuts and Seeds:**
  Rich in healthy fats, protein, fiber, and antioxidants. They help lower cholesterol, support heart health, and have anti-inflammatory properties.

- ✓ **Berries:**
  Berries such as blueberries, raspberries, and strawberries are packed with vitamins, minerals, and antioxidants that can help combat inflammation and chronic diseases.

- ✓ **Leafy Green Vegetables:**
  Spinach, kale, and arugula are rich in vitamins, minerals, and fiber, supporting digestive and immune health.

- ✓ **Garlic:**
  Has antibacterial and anti-inflammatory properties, supports the immune system, and helps regulate blood pressure.

- ✓ **Turmeric:**
  Known for its powerful anti-inflammatory and antioxidant properties. It can help protect against heart disease and cancers.

- ✓ **Flaxseed:**
  It is a rich source of omega-3 fatty acids, including linolenic, palmitic, oleic, and stearic acids, which help prevent cardiovascular diseases and lower cholesterol levels. It also reduces blood sugar levels, supports intestinal function, and has anti-cancer properties.

- ✓ **Green Tea:**
  Rich in catechins, which are strong antioxidants. It boosts metabolism, improves brain function, and supports heart health.

Functional Food Additives – Bioactive Ingredients

Bioactive ingredients, although usually not nutritional in value, positively affect our body's condition. The most commonly added to functional foods include:

- ✓ **Dietary Fiber:**
  Influences the digestive system, prevents constipation, regulates blood glucose levels, and counteracts colon cancer. Sources: whole grain products, seeds, legumes, fruits, and vegetables.

- ✓ **Prebiotics:**
  Stimulate gut bacteria, lower cholesterol levels, and prevent constipation. Natural prebiotics include inulin, raffinose, and oligofructose.

- ✓ **Probiotics:**
  Beneficial microorganisms that support the intestines, lower cholesterol, and strengthen the immune system. Examples: Lactobacillus rhamnosus, Lactobacillus acidophilus.

- ✓ **Amino Acids, Peptides, and Proteins:**
  Regulate metabolism, build tissues, and support mineral absorption. Examples: carnitine, taurine, essential amino acids such as leucine, valine, isoleucine.

- ✓ **Polyunsaturated Fatty Acids (PUFAs):**
  Have anti-inflammatory properties, support the heart and circulatory system. Sources of Omega-3: fatty fish, flaxseed oil; Omega-6: nuts, plant oils.

- ✓ **Vitamins:**
  Regulate metabolism, strengthen immunity, and act as antioxidants. Added vitamins include A, C, E, and D.

- ✓ **Minerals:**
  Strengthen immunity, mineralize bones, and regulate metabolism. Examples: calcium, magnesium, iron, zinc, selenium, iodine.

- ✓ **Choline:**
  Prevents fat accumulation in arteries, supports memory. Used as pure choline or in forms like choline chloride, citrate, and bitartrate.

- ✓ **Lecithin:**
  A component of cell membranes, prevents fatty liver, lowers bad cholesterol. Added to chocolate and baked goods.

- ✓ **Phytochemicals:**
  Support the immune system, act as antioxidants, and reduce oxidative stress. Examples: caffeine, flavonoids, glycosides.

- ✓ **Flavonoids:**
  Have antioxidant, antibacterial, and antiviral properties. Strengthen blood vessels and support vitamin C. Sources: cocoa, green tea, apricots, red wine.

- ✓ **Plant Sterols (Phytosterols):**
  Lower bad cholesterol, found in plant oils, nuts, seeds, and almonds.

Bioactive ingredients support health and improve the quality of life by providing essential components that positively influence bodily functions.

Fortified Functional Foods

- ✓ **Probiotic Yogurts:**
  Contain beneficial bacteria that support gut health and the immune system.

- ✓ **Natural Juices with Added Vitamins and Minerals:**
  For example, orange juice fortified with calcium and vitamin D to support bone health. It is important that these juices are not sweetened with sugar.

- ✓ **Muesli Enriched with Vitamins and Minerals:**
  Can support digestive health and help control blood sugar levels.

Health Benefits of Functional Foods

- ***Immune System Support***

  Probiotics: Probiotic bacteria in yogurts can improve gut health, which is crucial for a strong immune system.

  Antioxidants: Substances such as vitamin C, vitamin E, and polyphenols in fruits and vegetables help combat free radicals and support immunity.

- ***Improved Heart Health***

  Omega-3 Fatty Acids: Found in fish, flaxseeds, and walnuts, they can help lower cholesterol levels and reduce inflammation.

  Fiber: Present in whole grain products and legumes, fiber helps lower cholesterol levels and supports heart health.

- ***Digestive Health***

  Soluble and Insoluble Fiber: Found in fruits, vegetables, whole grains, and legumes, supports regular bowel movements and gut health.

  Probiotics and Prebiotics: Probiotics support a healthy gut flora, while prebiotics, such as inulin, provide nourishment for beneficial gut bacteria.

- ***Support for Brain and Cognitive Function***

  Omega-3 Fatty Acids: Important for brain health, they can improve cognitive functions and reduce the risk of neurodegenerative disorders.

  Antioxidants: Help protect brain cells from oxidative stress.

Incorporating Functional Foods into Your Diet

To fully benefit from the health advantages of functional foods, it's important to incorporate a variety of products that provide a wide range of nutrients. Here are some tips on how to do this:

⇨ **Include a Variety of Fruits and Vegetables in Your Daily Diet:**
Aim to have as many colors as possible on your plate – a diversity of colors means a diversity of nutrients.

⇨ **Swap Snacks for Healthy Alternatives:**
Instead of chips or sweets, opt for nuts, seeds, or fruits.

⇨ **Choose Whole Grain Products:**
Whole grain bread, pasta, and rice are richer in fiber and nutrients than their refined counterparts.

⇨ **Consume Fortified Products:**
Select foods fortified with vitamins and minerals to help fill potential gaps in your diet.

Scientific Research on Functional Foods

Studies on functional foods show that regularly consuming nutrient-rich products can bring numerous health benefits. For example, research published in the *American Journal of Clinical Nutrition* found that consuming nuts can lower the risk of cardiovascular diseases. Other studies published in the *Journal of Nutrition* indicate that probiotics can improve gut health and support the immune system.

Short Summary - My Daily Life

Functional foods are an excellent way to enrich your diet and support your health in a natural and delicious manner. Incorporating these products into your daily menu can improve your well-being, boost immunity, and support overall health and fitness.

When shopping and reading product labels, we are essentially choosing what we eat. It's up to us to decide whether to choose foods enriched with additives or not. Sometimes we consume them without even knowing. It's truly worth spending a bit more time on shopping rather than wasting time scrolling through social media. This will bring tremendous benefits to our health.

Now, let's look into another important issue mentioned earlier, namely supplementation. Is it necessary, or is it just another marketing ploy to make us spend more money?

CHAPTER 22

Supplementation – When, What, and For Whom?

Dietary supplementation is becoming increasingly popular, especially in the context of growing health awareness. However, with the vast array of products available, it's important to know which supplements are truly necessary, how to use them correctly, and what potential risks may be associated with them. In this chapter, we will discuss the most important aspects of supplementation to help you make informed health choices.

Why Use Supplements?

Dietary supplements can be useful in various situations, such as:

- ⇨ **Vitamin and mineral deficiencies** resulting from a diet lacking these essential nutrients.
- ⇨ **Increased nutrient needs** in specific physiological states, such as pregnancy, breastfeeding, intense physical training, or aging.
- ⇨ **Special health needs**, such as supporting the immune system, bone health, or improving cognitive functions.

How Deficiencies of Specific Vitamins and Minerals Affect Health

Vitamin and mineral deficiencies can lead to various health problems. Here's an overview of how the lack of these key nutrients can impact our health:

- ***Vitamin A:***
  Essential for healthy vision, skin, and immune function. Deficiency can lead to vision problems such as night blindness, weakened immune system, and dry skin.

- ***Vitamin B1 (Thiamine):***
  Crucial for carbohydrate metabolism and nerve function. Deficiency can cause beriberi, weakness, nervous system problems, and decreased concentration.

- ***Vitamin B2 (Riboflavin):***
  Important for healthy skin, eyes, and nerve functions. Deficiency can lead to cracked corners of the mouth, inflamed tongue, skin irritation, and eye fatigue.

- ***Vitamin B3 (Niacin):***
  Helps with energy metabolism and skin health. Deficiency can cause pellagra, which includes symptoms such as skin lesions, diarrhea, dementia, and mood changes.

- ***Vitamin B5 (Pantothenic Acid):***
  Essential for energy metabolism. Deficiency can lead to fatigue, headaches, irritability, and sleep disturbances.

- ***Vitamin B6 (Pyridoxine):***
  Important for amino acid metabolism and nervous system health. Deficiency can cause depression, skin irritation, anemia, and muscle cramps.

- ***Vitamin B7 (Biotin):***
  Key for healthy hair, skin, and nails. Deficiency can lead to hair loss, skin rashes, and nervous system problems.

- ***Vitamin B9 (Folic Acid):***
  Essential for DNA synthesis and blood health. Deficiency can cause megaloblastic anemia, birth defects in infants, and digestive issues.

- ***Vitamin B12 (Cobalamin):***
  Important for nerve function and blood formation. Deficiency can cause anemia, fatigue, neurological problems, and balance disorders.

- ***Vitamin C:***
  Crucial for collagen synthesis, skin health, and immune functions. Deficiency can lead to scurvy, weakness, bleeding gums, and delayed wound healing.

- ***Vitamin D:***
  Important for bone health and the immune system. Deficiency can lead to osteoporosis, weakened bones, and reduced immunity.

- ***Vitamin E:***
  Acts as an antioxidant, protecting cells from damage. Deficiency can cause nervous system problems, muscle weakness, and impaired vision.

- ***Vitamin K:***

  Essential for blood clotting and bone health. Deficiency can lead to blood clotting issues and weakened bones.

- ***Calcium:***

  Vital for bone, teeth, and muscle function. Deficiency can lead to weakened bones, osteoporosis, and muscle cramps.

- ***Magnesium:***

  Important for muscle function, the nervous system, and cardiovascular health. Deficiency can lead to muscle cramps, weakness, nervous system problems, and migraines.

- ***Iron:***

  Crucial for the formation of red blood cells and oxygen transport. Deficiency can lead to anemia, fatigue, weakness, and shortness of breath.

- ***Zinc:***

  Important for the immune system, wound healing, and DNA synthesis. Deficiency can lead to weakened immunity, wound healing issues, and disturbances in taste and smell.

- ***Selenium:***

  Key for thyroid function and antioxidant protection. Deficiency can lead to thyroid problems, weakened immunity, and cardiomyopathy.

- ***Iodine:***

  Essential for thyroid function and metabolism. Deficiency can lead to thyroid issues, goiter, and fatigue.

- ***Copper:***
  Important for the formation of red blood cells, nerve health, and the immune system. Deficiency can lead to anemia, nervous system problems, and skin changes.

- ***Manganese:***
  Crucial for metabolism and bone health. Deficiency can lead to bone and joint issues and fertility problems.

- ***Chromium:***
  Essential for glucose metabolism and insulin function. Deficiency can lead to glucose metabolism issues, elevated blood sugar levels, and mood swings.

- ***Molybdenum:***
  Important for amino acid metabolism and antioxidant protection. Deficiency can lead to amino acid metabolism issues and weakened immunity.

- ***Potassium:***
  Key for electrolyte balance, muscle function, and the nervous system. Deficiency can lead to blood pressure issues, muscle weakness, and heart rhythm disturbances.

- ***Sodium:***
  Essential for electrolyte balance and nerve function. Deficiency can lead to electrolyte imbalance and blood pressure issues.

- ***Phosphorus:***
  Important for bone and teeth health and energy metabolism. Deficiency can lead to bone issues, muscle weakness, and cognitive function disturbances.

- ***Sulfur:***
  Crucial for the health of hair, skin, and nails. Deficiency can lead to problems with hair, skin, nails, and joint pain.

- ***Silicon:***
  Important for bone health, joint function, and skin elasticity. Deficiency can lead to bone, joint, skin, hair, and nail issues, and reduced skin elasticity.

- ***Boron:***
  A trace element that plays a key role in various metabolic processes and is essential for bone health and proper hormonal function.

- ***Lecithin:***
  Deficiency can lead to fatty liver, elevated levels of bad cholesterol, and memory problems. Lecithin is important for liver health, lipid metabolism, and brain function.

How Deficiencies of Specific Fatty Acids Affect Health

- ***Omega-3 Fatty Acids:***
  A deficiency in omega-3 can lead to memory and concentration issues, dry skin and hair, joint pain, and an increased risk of inflammation. Omega-3 is crucial for brain, heart, and circulatory health.

- ***Omega-6 Fatty Acids:***
  Deficiency in omega-6 manifests as dry, flaky skin, growth problems in children, weakened immune system, and fertility issues. Maintaining a proper balance between omega-3 and omega-6 is important.

- ***Omega-9 Fatty Acids:***
  A deficiency in omega-9 can lead to heart and circulatory system problems. Omega-9 supports cholesterol levels and improves blood sugar control.

- ***Monounsaturated Fatty Acids (MUFA):***
  Deficiency in monounsaturated fatty acids increases the risk of heart disease, problems with blood sugar regulation, and dry skin. MUFAs are important for heart health and blood sugar regulation.

- ***Saturated Fatty Acids:***
  A deficiency in saturated fatty acids can cause brain function problems, issues with the absorption of fat-soluble vitamins (A, D, E, K), and a weakened immune system. Saturated fatty acids are important for brain health and the immune system.

The Importance of Supplement Quality

Not all dietary supplements are created equal, and their quality can vary significantly depending on the manufacturer. High-quality supplements are more effective and safer for health.

Several factors influence the bioavailability of dietary supplements, which is important to understand for optimal supplementation. The supplement formula plays a crucial role, as some forms of nutrients are better absorbed than others. For instance, liquid forms or capsules may be more effective than tablets.

The composition of a meal is another important aspect; fat-soluble vitamins such as A, D, E, and K are best absorbed in the presence of fats. On the other hand, iron absorption can be disrupted by dairy, coffee, or tea. Interactions with other substances also matter; calcium supplements can hinder iron absorption, so it's advisable to wait two hours between taking them. Another example is vitamin D, which enhances calcium absorption from the digestive tract, but vitamin K2 is helpful in directing calcium to bone tissue, preventing vascular calcification and strengthening bone structure.

Gastrointestinal health is equally important – low stomach acid secretion affects the absorption of vitamin B12, and intestinal inflammation can disrupt the absorption of folates and other nutrients.

The best supplements come from natural, high-quality sources, as synthetic versions of vitamins and minerals may be less effective. It's also important to choose supplements free from artificial additives, preservatives, and fillers. Quality certifications are an important indicator; look for supplements with certifications from independent organizations confirming their quality and purity. Choose supplements whose efficacy has been proven in scientific studies. Trusted brands with good reputations are more likely to offer high-quality products. Understanding these factors can help optimize supplementation and improve health.

Avoid Store Shelf Supplements

Many supplements available on store shelves may contain low-quality ingredients, artificial additives, and fillers. Instead, it's worth investing in products from trusted sources that offer the highest quality and effectiveness. Remember that price often correlates with quality—cheap supplements may not provide the expected health benefits.

Short Summary - My Daily Life

In my daily routine, there is always a place for supplementation, which is a vital complement to my diet. Since I incorporated regular supplementation, I haven't had any immune system issues—I don't get sick even during the fall-winter season or when I'm around sick people. I also don't experience bone or joint problems, concentration issues, or fatigue.

Dietary supplements can be a valuable addition to a healthy diet, but their quality is crucial. By choosing high-quality supplements, we can ensure that we are providing our bodies with essential nutrients in the most effective form. Investing in good supplements is an investment in our health. However, it is important to choose supplements individually based on personal needs, ideally consulting with a knowledgeable professional. Equally important is the proper combination of supplements to ensure their optimal bioavailability and to avoid potential interactions that could affect their effectiveness.

PART VIII

THE MICRO WORLD WITHIN US

CHAPTER 23

Microbiome and Probiotics - Allies in Our Gut

The microbiome, a collection of microorganisms inhabiting our bodies, plays a crucial role in our health and well-being. Our intestines host a vast number of bacteria, viruses, fungi, and other microorganisms that form a complex ecosystem. These microorganisms are essential for proper digestion, the production of certain vitamins, and protection against pathogens.

Probiotics are beneficial bacteria that support the health of our microbiome. They are available in supplement form as well as in natural fermented products such as yogurts, kefirs, pickles, and kombucha.

The Importance of the Microbiome

The gut microbiome, a collection of microorganisms inhabiting our intestines, plays a crucial role in many aspects of health. Its influence extends far beyond digestion, affecting the immune system, metabolism, and even mental health. The intestines host billions of different bacteria, viruses, and fungi that work together with our bodies, supporting digestive processes and vitamin synthesis, while also protecting against pathogens.

Disruptions in the balance of the microbiome, known as dysbiosis, can lead to numerous health problems. Increasing research indicates a connection between dysbiosis and autoimmune diseases such as Crohn's disease, ulcerative colitis, and rheumatoid arthritis. An improper balance of microorganisms can also lead to obesity and type 2 diabetes by affecting metabolism and fat storage. A study conducted by the University of Copenhagen found that supplementation with the probiotic Lactobacillus rhamnosus GG reduces inflammation and improves gut health in patients with Crohn's disease.

The Impact of the Microbiome on Mental Health

The influence of the microbiome on mental health is another fascinating area of research. Studies show that the gut microbiome can affect the production of neurotransmitters, such as serotonin, which directly impacts mood and anxiety levels. Disruptions in the microbiome may be linked to depression, anxiety, and other mental health issues.

A study published in the journal "Psychological Medicine" found that supplementation with probiotics (Bifidobacterium longum) for six weeks significantly reduced symptoms of depression in patients with irritable bowel syndrome (IBS).

The Benefits of Probiotics

Probiotics, beneficial live microorganisms, play a crucial role in maintaining a healthy gut microbiome. Regular consumption of probiotics offers numerous advantages that impact various aspects of our health. Here are some of the key benefits:

⇨ **Supporting Gut Health:**
Probiotics help maintain the balance of the gut microbiome, which is essential for healthy digestion and regular bowel movements. A balanced gut microbiome supports proper digestive function, preventing issues such as constipation, diarrhea, and irritable bowel syndrome (IBS). Beneficial probiotic bacteria like Lactobacillus and Bifidobacterium aid in the breakdown and absorption of nutrients and the production of short-chain fatty acids that nourish gut cells.

⇨ **Boosting the Immune System:**
Probiotics can enhance the body's resistance to infections by supporting antibody production and strengthening the gut barrier. A robust gut microbiome acts as the first line of defense against pathogens, preventing them from penetrating the gut wall into the bloodstream. Regular probiotic intake can also increase the activity of immune cells, such as macrophages and lymphocytes, helping to fight infections and diseases.

A study published in the "Journal of Clinical Gastroenterology" found that probiotics (Lactobacillus casei) significantly reduced the frequency of respiratory tract infections in preschool children.

⇨ **Improving Mental Health:**
Research suggests that a healthy microbiome can positively impact mental health by reducing symptoms of depression and anxiety. The gut-brain axis, or the communication between the gut and the brain, plays a crucial role in regulating mood and cognitive functions. Probiotics can influence the production of neurotransmitters such as serotonin, which is associated with feelings of happiness and calm. Additionally, probiotics can

reduce inflammation in the body, which is important for mental health, as chronic inflammation is linked to depression and other mood disorders.

How to Incorporate Probiotics into Your Diet

To reap the benefits of probiotics, it's important to include foods rich in these beneficial microorganisms in your diet. Here are some examples:

- ✓ **Yogurts and Kefirs:**
  These are natural sources of probiotics that can be consumed daily as part of a healthy breakfast or snack.

- ✓ **Fermented Vegetables:**
  Sauerkraut, kimchi, pickles, and other fermented vegetables are excellent sources of probiotics.

- ✓ **Fermented Beet Juice:**
  Fermented beet juice has enhanced antioxidant properties, supports gut health, and serves as a natural probiotic that can be used daily to help manage various health conditions.

- ✓ **Tempeh:**
  A fermented soybean product that can be added to salads, soups, and main dishes.

- ✓ **Miso:**
  A fermented soybean paste, perfect for preparing soups and sauces.

- ✓ **Kombucha:**
  A fermented tea drink that serves as a refreshing alternative to other beverages.

Incorporating these probiotic-rich foods into your daily diet can help maintain a healthy gut microbiome, support digestion, and boost overall health.

How Deficiencies of Specific Probiotics Affect Health

Probiotics play a crucial role in maintaining a healthy gut microbiome, which is the foundation of overall health. Deficiencies in specific probiotic strains can lead to various health issues, affecting both the digestive and immune systems. Here are some examples of how individual probiotic strains affect health and the consequences of their deficiency:

- ***Lactobacillus acidophilus:***
  Deficiency in Lactobacillus acidophilus can lead to digestive issues such as bloating, diarrhea, and constipation. It can also affect vaginal health in women, leading to yeast and bacterial infections. Lactobacillus acidophilus supports the immune system and helps synthesize B vitamins.

- ***Bifidobacterium bifidum:***
  A deficiency in Bifidobacterium bifidum can cause digestive problems and an increased risk of diarrhea. It can also affect gut health, leading to irritable bowel syndrome (IBS). Bifidobacterium bifidum supports the balance of gut microflora, helps in carbohydrate digestion, and synthesizes B vitamins.

- ***Lactobacillus rhamnosus:***
  Deficiency in Lactobacillus rhamnosus can lead to reduced immunity, increased risk of infections, and digestive issues. It can also affect mental health, as there is a connection between gut microbiota and brain health. Lactobacillus rhamnosus supports

gut health, boosts immunity, and may reduce symptoms of anxiety and depression.

- ***Lactobacillus reuteri:***
  Deficiency in Lactobacillus reuteri can lead to digestive problems such as bloating and diarrhea, and reduced immunity. Lactobacillus reuteri supports oral health, urinary tract health, and improves the overall balance of gut microflora.

- ***Bifidobacterium longum:***
  Deficiency in Bifidobacterium longum can cause digestive problems, including constipation and bloating. It can also affect mental health, increasing the risk of anxiety and depression. Bifidobacterium longum supports gut health, reduces inflammation, and can improve mood.

- ***Saccharomyces boulardii:***
  Deficiency in Saccharomyces boulardii can lead to digestive issues such as antibiotic-induced or infection-induced diarrhea. It can also affect gut health, increasing the risk of yeast infections. Saccharomyces boulardii supports gut health, helps treat diarrhea, and boosts the immune system.

- ***Lactobacillus plantarum:***
  Deficiency in Lactobacillus plantarum can lead to digestive problems and reduced immunity. It can also affect skin health, increasing the risk of inflammation and skin infections. Lactobacillus plantarum supports gut health, reduces inflammation, and improves skin health.

- ***Bifidobacterium lactis:***
  Deficiency in Bifidobacterium lactis can cause digestive problems and reduced immunity. It can also affect bone health by reducing calcium absorption. Bifidobacterium lactis supports gut health, boosts immunity, and aids in the absorption of minerals.

Short Summary - My Daily Life

Regular consumption of probiotics can help maintain a healthy gut microbiome and provide numerous health benefits. I personally include probiotics in my daily diet. It's important to remember that diversity is key to a healthy microbiome, so incorporating various sources of probiotics into your diet is beneficial.

We have already discussed how the microbiome and probiotics can significantly impact our health, supporting not only digestion but also the immune system and mental health. A healthy microbiome is the foundation of overall well-being. However, probiotics are just one piece of the larger puzzle of a healthy diet.

In the next chapter, we will explore how a holistic healthy diet can become a key element in treating and preventing many diseases. We will understand which nutrients and dietary habits support healing processes and help maintain optimal health.

Fun Fact: Check Your Gut Health with the Beet Test

Did you know that you can perform a simple at-home test to assess the integrity of your gut using a beet? Simply eat a beet or drink beet juice and observe the color of your urine within a few hours. If you notice a pink or reddish tint, it might suggest that the pigments from the beet have passed through a leaky gut into your bloodstream. This could be a sign that it's time to take a closer look at your gut microbiome and consider making dietary changes and adding probiotics to support its balance.

If the test results indicate possible gut issues, it's advisable to consult a qualified specialist who can help accurately diagnose the state of your gut microbiome and provide personalized therapy to support your gut health.

CHAPTER 24

A Healthy Diet as a Path to Healing

A healthy diet is not only a way to maintain good physical condition but also a powerful tool in treating and preventing many diseases. A well-balanced diet can support the body's regenerative processes, strengthen the immune system, and improve overall well-being. Let's consider how a healthy diet can act as a support in combating various ailments.

Supporting the Cardiovascular System

A diet rich in healthy fats, such as those from fish, nuts, olive oil, and avocados, can help lower bad cholesterol (LDL) and increase good cholesterol (HDL). Consuming plenty of fruits, vegetables, whole grains, and avoiding trans fats and excess salt can reduce the risk of heart disease and hypertension. Here are some examples of heart-healthy foods:

- ✓ **Salmon**: Rich in omega-3 fatty acids, supports heart health.
- ✓ **Walnuts**: Contain healthy fats and antioxidants.
- ✓ **Olive oil**: A healthy fat that lowers cholesterol levels.
- ✓ **Avocado**: Full of healthy fats and fiber.
- ✓ **Spinach**: Rich in vitamins and minerals.

Supporting Diabetes Management

A low glycemic index diet, rich in fiber, plant-based protein, and healthy fats, can help manage blood sugar levels. Fruits, vegetables, whole grains, nuts, and seeds are key components of a diabetes-friendly diet. Avoiding processed foods, sugary drinks, and excess simple carbohydrates is equally important. Here are examples of healthy foods for managing diabetes:

- ✓ **Quinoa**: Rich in protein and fiber, with a low glycemic index.
- ✓ **Berries**: Low in calories and high in antioxidants.
- ✓ **Chickpeas**: An excellent source of plant-based protein.
- ✓ **Eggs**: High in protein and healthy fats.
- ✓ **Nuts**: Full of healthy fats and fiber.

Boosting the Immune System

A healthy diet rich in vitamins, minerals, and antioxidants can strengthen the immune system. Vitamin C (found in citrus fruits, peppers, broccoli), vitamin D (in fatty fish, egg yolks), zinc (in nuts, seeds, meat), and selenium (in Brazil nuts, fish) play crucial roles in maintaining strong immunity. Here are examples of healthy foods that support the immune system:

- ✓ **Oranges**: A rich source of vitamin C.
- ✓ **Broccoli**: Packed with vitamins and antioxidants.
- ✓ **Brazil nuts**: An excellent source of selenium.
- ✓ **Red bell peppers**: High in vitamin C.
- ✓ **Yogurt**: A natural source of probiotics.

Improving Mental Health

A healthy diet can also positively impact mental health. Fruits, vegetables, whole grains, fatty fish, nuts, and seeds are rich in nutrients that support brain health. Omega-3 fatty acids from fish, antioxidants from berries, and magnesium from leafy green vegetables can help reduce inflammation and improve mood, which is essential in preventing depression and anxiety. Here are some examples of healthy foods that support mental health:

- ✓ **Spinach**: Rich in magnesium, supports mental health.
- ✓ **Almonds**: Excellent source of magnesium and healthy fats.
- ✓ **Berries**: Full of antioxidants, support brain health.
- ✓ **Bananas**: Source of B vitamins and potassium.
- ✓ **Walnuts**: Rich in omega-3, support brain health.

Fighting Cancer

Certain dietary components can help protect against cancer. Cruciferous vegetables (broccoli, cauliflower, cabbage) contain sulfur compounds that aid in detoxifying the body and may reduce cancer risk. A diet high in fiber, fruits, vegetables, and whole grains can help maintain a healthy weight and reduce the risk of colorectal cancer. Here are examples of healthy foods that help fight cancer:

- ✓ **Broccoli**: Contains sulforaphane, which may protect against cancer.
- ✓ **Carrots**: Rich in beta-carotene, a powerful antioxidant.
- ✓ **Beans**: High in fiber, support gut health.
- ✓ **Cabbage**: Full of sulfur compounds.
- ✓ **Garlic**: Contains allicin, which has anti-cancer properties.

Improving Gut Health

A healthy diet also supports gut health. Consuming fermented products such as yogurt, kefir, sauerkraut, and kimchi provides probiotics that support a healthy gut microbiome. Fiber from fruits, vegetables, and whole grains acts as a prebiotic, nourishing beneficial bacteria in the gut. Here are some examples of healthy foods that support gut health:

- ✓ **Kefir**: Rich in probiotics, supports gut health.
- ✓ **Sauerkraut**: A natural source of probiotics.
- ✓ **Bananas**: High in fiber and prebiotics, support gut health.
- ✓ **Apples**: A source of fiber and pectin.
- ✓ **Leafy Green Vegetables**: Full of fiber and antioxidants.

Short Summary - My Daily Life

Food plays a crucial role in our lives, being a daily necessity. I believe it should never be boring or tasteless but diverse, nutritionally balanced, and above all, delicious. The key is balance and variety, as well as avoiding processed foods and excessive sugars and trans fats. By maintaining a healthy diet, we can improve our quality of life and protect our health in the long term.

Planning a healthy menu doesn't have to be difficult or monotonous. Each day can be different, and a variety of nutrients and flavors will make the diet not only healthy but also enjoyable. Create a plan that best suits your preferences.

In the previously mentioned book, ***"Sugar, Gluten, and Dairy-Free Recipes"*** you'll find ideas for breakfasts, lunches, dinners, and desserts.

For example, a vegetable omelet for breakfast can be paired with a grilled chicken salad for lunch or dinner. Similarly, you can opt for a berry and plant protein smoothie as a snack and baked fish with vegetables for dinner.

Experiment with different combinations to discover new tastes and health benefits.

PART IX

FOOD AND COSMETICS

CHAPTER 25

What We Put on Our Skin Affects Our Health

Our dietary choices influence not only our internal health but also the appearance and condition of our skin. Just as we are mindful of what we eat, we should also pay attention to what we apply to our skin. Cosmetics, like food, can contain ingredients that have a direct impact on our health. What we put on our skin penetrates our body, so it's important to choose products with natural, healthy ingredients.

The Impact of Cosmetic Ingredients on Health

The skin is the largest organ of our body and acts as a protective barrier. However, not all cosmetic ingredients are neutral to our health. Some can penetrate the skin and enter the bloodstream, affecting the functioning of the body. Below are some common cosmetic ingredients that may have negative health effects:

- **Parabens**
  Parabens are widely used as preservatives in cosmetics to prevent the growth of bacteria and mold. While they effectively extend the shelf life of products, they can disrupt hormonal function. Studies

suggest that parabens can mimic estrogen, potentially leading to hormonal imbalances and increasing the risk of breast cancer.

- **Phthalates**

  Phthalates are used to prolong the shelf life of fragrances in cosmetics and as plasticizers in hair styling products. These chemicals can impact the endocrine and reproductive systems. Research indicates that phthalates can reduce sperm quality in men and cause early puberty in girls.

- **Sulfates**

  Sulfates, such as sodium lauryl sulfate (SLS) and ammonium lauryl sulfate (SLES), are commonly found in shampoos, body washes, and toothpastes. Although effective at removing dirt and oils, they can irritate and dry out the skin. Prolonged use of sulfate-containing products can lead to skin problems like eczema and flaking.

- **Aluminum**

  Research shows that aluminum in antiperspirants can damage DNA, potentially leading to breast cancer, particularly in the underarm area. Experts also see a connection between the use of spray antiperspirants and an increased susceptibility to Alzheimer's disease.

- **Fluoride**

  While fluoride is effective in preventing tooth decay, excessive intake can have negative health effects, and we brush our teeth multiple times a day. Dental fluorosis manifests as white spots on teeth, which can lead to discoloration and enamel damage. Excess fluoride can cause bone problems, such as skeletal fluorosis, leading to weakened bones and joints and an increased risk of fractures. Fluoride can also disrupt thyroid function, lowering hormone production, which affects metabolism and well-being. High levels of fluoride can impact neurological development in children, causing issues with IQ and cognitive functions. Excessive fluoride can cause neurodegeneration in the cerebellum, hippocampus, and cortex. It negatively affects neurotransmitter synthesis and their receptors in the brain. Chronic exposure to high doses of fluoride is also harmful to the muscular and reproductive systems, increasing the risk of infertility and miscarriages, as well as susceptibility to Alzheimer's disease. Remember that we also ingest fluoride through water.

The Importance of Conscious Cosmetic Choices

A conscious approach to selecting cosmetics is crucial for maintaining healthy skin and overall health. Here are some tips on how to avoid harmful ingredients and choose safe products:

⇨ **Read Labels:**
Pay attention to the ingredients listed on product labels. Avoid cosmetics that contain parabens, phthalates, sulfates, aluminum, and fluoride.

⇨ **Choose Natural Products:**
Opt for cosmetics with natural ingredients, which are less likely to cause irritation and allergic reactions. Many cosmetic companies now offer lines of products that are safe for both skin and the environment.

⇨ **Look for Certifications:**
Eco-friendly and organic certifications can help identify safe products. Certified products are usually free from harmful chemicals and have been tested for safety.

⇨ **Test Before Use:**
Before applying a new cosmetic product all over your body, conduct a patch test on a small area of skin to ensure it does not cause an allergic reaction.

How to Choose Healthy Cosmetics

When selecting cosmetics, it is essential to pay attention to the ingredients and avoid products containing potentially harmful chemicals. The modern cosmetics market is vast, so a conscious approach to shopping is key. Be mindful of ingredients like parabens, phthalates, silicones, sulfates, and synthetic fragrances, which can negatively impact health.

⇨ **Look for Eco and Organic Certifications:**
Seeking eco-friendly and organic certifications can help identify safe products. Certifications such as ECOCERT, COSMOS, and USDA Organic ensure that products are made according to strict standards, reducing the risk of allergic reactions and irritations. These certifications often indicate that the products do not contain artificial colors, preservatives, and other harmful substances.

⇨ **Read Labels Carefully:**
Reading labels and making informed cosmetic choices can significantly impact the health of your skin and overall body. It's worth taking the time to understand what lies behind complex

ingredient names. Natural substances, such as plant oils, herbal extracts, and beeswax, are generally safer and more skin-friendly.

⇨ **Consider Skin Sensitivity:**
Remember that not all natural ingredients are safe for everyone. Individuals with sensitive skin should avoid essential oils, which can cause irritation. Testing new products on a small skin patch before full use can help avoid unpleasant surprises.

Natural Ingredients in Cosmetics

More and more people are turning to natural and organic cosmetics that utilize plant-based and mineral ingredients. These products are not only gentler on the skin but also often more effective in the long term. Here are some examples of natural ingredients worth incorporating into your daily skincare routine:

✓ **Coconut Oil**
Coconut oil is excellent for moisturizing the skin and hair. It has antibacterial and antifungal properties, helping to combat bacteria and microbes that can cause breakouts and other skin issues. Rich in fatty acids, it helps keep the skin smooth and soft. It can be used as a body lotion, hair conditioner, or even as a makeup remover.

✓ **Aloe Vera**
Aloe vera is known for its soothing and moisturizing properties. Aloe gel is ideal for sensitive and irritated skin, helping to alleviate redness, burning, and itching. It also supports skin regeneration, making it effective for treating minor cuts and burns. Aloe can be found in creams, face masks, and toners.

- ✓ **Shea Butter**

  Shea butter is rich in vitamins A and E, essential for maintaining healthy skin. It deeply moisturizes and regenerates the skin, enhancing its elasticity and firmness. Often used in hand creams, body lotions, and lip balms, shea butter helps combat dry and chapped skin, leaving it soft and smooth.

- ✓ **Argan Oil**

  Known as "liquid gold," argan oil is rich in unsaturated fatty acids and vitamin E. Its strong moisturizing and nourishing properties make it ideal for dry and aging skin. Argan oil can be applied to the face, body, and hair, giving them a healthy shine and appearance.

- ✓ **Honey**

  Honey is a natural humectant, meaning it attracts moisture to the skin. Its antibacterial and anti-inflammatory properties make it an excellent ingredient for acne-prone and irritated skin. Honey can be found in face masks, balms, and scrubs, where it helps to moisturize, nourish, and soothe the skin.

- ✓ **Tea Tree Oil**

  Tea tree oil is known for its antibacterial and anti-inflammatory properties. It is effective in treating acne and other skin issues by combating bacteria and reducing inflammation. This oil can be applied directly to pimples or added to toners and masks.

- ✓ **Chamomile Extract**

  Chamomile extract is commonly used in cosmetics for sensitive and irritated skin. It has soothing, anti-inflammatory, and antiseptic properties. Chamomile extract can be found in creams, micellar waters, and toners, helping to calm the skin and reduce redness.

- ✓ **Natural Argan Oil Shampoo**
  This shampoo perfectly moisturizes and regenerates even the most damaged hair, making it shiny and strong.

- ✓ **Natural Bath Gels and Liquids**
  Containing natural ingredients like flavonoids—extracts from sloe flowers with strengthening and antioxidant properties—or cinnamon oil with firming properties, these bath products invigorate and visibly improve skin condition.

Natural ingredients in cosmetics offer a range of benefits that can improve our skin's condition without the risks associated with synthetic additives. By choosing products with coconut oil, aloe, shea butter, honey, and other natural ingredients, we can ensure healthy, radiant skin while caring for our health and the environment. Investing in cosmetics based on natural ingredients allows us to enjoy their beneficial effects in the long run.

DIY Cosmetics: A Natural Alternative

An alternative to store-bought cosmetics can be DIY (do it yourself) products that you can prepare at home using natural ingredients. Making your own cosmetics is not only a fun activity but also a healthy and safe way to take care of yourself. With just a few simple ingredients, often found in your kitchen, you can create effective and enjoyable cosmetics.

- ✓ **Avocado Masks**
  Avocado is a true vitamin bomb for your skin. It is rich in healthy fats, vitamins E and C, and antioxidants that nourish and

moisturize the skin. To prepare an avocado mask, simply mash half of a ripe avocado and apply it to a cleansed face. You can add a teaspoon of honey for its antibacterial and additional moisturizing properties. Leave the mask on for 15-20 minutes, then rinse with warm water.

✓ **Sugar and Essential Oil Scrubs**
Scrubs are great for removing dead skin cells and leaving the skin smooth and radiant. One of the simplest DIY scrubs is a sugar scrub. Mix half a cup of sugar (brown or cane) with a few tablespoons of coconut oil or olive oil. Add a few drops of your favorite essential oil, such as lavender or orange, to give the scrub a pleasant scent. Gently massage the scrub onto your skin for a few minutes, then rinse with warm water.

✓ **Green Tea Toner**
Green tea is full of antioxidants that help protect the skin from harmful external factors and have anti-inflammatory properties. To prepare a green tea toner, brew a strong infusion using two bags of green tea and let it cool. Then pour the infusion into a spray bottle and store it in the refrigerator. This toner is excellent for refreshing the skin and helping fight acne. You can use it daily after washing your face.

By making your own cosmetics with these natural ingredients, you can ensure that you are using products that are safe, effective, and tailored to your skin's needs.

Benefits of DIY Cosmetics

Homemade cosmetics are not only cost-effective but also free from harmful chemicals often found in store-bought products. You know exactly what you are putting on your skin, which is particularly important if you have sensitive or allergy-prone skin. Additionally, making DIY cosmetics is a great way to relax and spend time creatively.

DIY cosmetics are an excellent alternative to commercial products. They are easy to make, economical, and natural. Try recipes for avocado masks, sugar scrubs, and green tea toners to enjoy healthy and beautiful skin without chemicals. Creating your own cosmetics can become your new, healthy passion!

Natural Cleaning Products

It's also important to pay attention to the cleaning products we use in our homes. Like cosmetics, these products can contain harmful chemicals that may affect our health. Choosing natural and eco-friendly cleaning products is just as crucial as being mindful of what we apply to our skin. Natural products are less harmful to our bodies and the environment while effectively maintaining cleanliness in our surroundings.

Chemicals in conventional cleaning products can negatively impact our health, causing allergies, skin irritations, and respiratory problems. Opting for natural cleaning agents such as vinegar, baking soda, essential oils, or bio products can be an effective and safe solution.

These products are not only less harmful to our health but also more environmentally friendly.

Introducing natural cleaning products into our daily cleaning routines is another step towards a healthier lifestyle. By doing so, we can minimize exposure to harmful substances and enjoy a clean, healthy home.

Short Summary - My Daily Life

Healthy eating and skincare go hand in hand. By taking care of what we consume and what we apply to our skin, we can ensure better health, well-being, and appearance. Personally, I haven't used antiperspirants or fluoride toothpaste for the past 10 years. I care for my complexion and skin naturally with vitamin C, vitamin E, and natural oils such as carrot oil, raspberry oil, castor oil, almond oil, and others. My body is moisturized and free from harmful substances, contributing to its healthy appearance and better well-being.

I also use natural products for cleaning the house and doing laundry. I made the change in one day, and now I buy larger packages of proven products, saving time and money.

Remember, everything natural is beneficial for our bodies both inside and out.

CHAPTER 26

Children's Health and Modern Nutritional Challenges

In today's rapidly changing world, children's eating habits are significantly influenced by globalization, technological advancements, and changes in lifestyle. Unfortunately, not all these changes are beneficial for the health of the youngest. Increasingly, children's diets are based on products high in sugar, such as cookies, yogurts, white bread, and fast food.

Impact of Processed Food

Processed food, often high in sugars, trans fats, and artificial additives, is widely available and affordable, making it an attractive option for many families. However, its regular consumption can have negative effects on children's health:

- ***Increased Incidence of Illnesses:***
  Consuming large amounts of processed food can lead to a higher frequency of lifestyle-related diseases.

- ***Behavioral and Learning Problems:***
  Studies suggest that a diet rich in sugars and artificial additives can

affect children's behavior, causing issues with concentration and learning.

The Impact of Food Quality on Children's Development

A healthy, balanced diet is crucial for the proper physical and mental development of children. Proper nutrition influences:

- ⇨ **Growth and Physical Development:**
  Proteins, vitamins, and minerals are essential for the proper growth of bones, muscles, and tissues.

- ⇨ **Brain Development:**
  Omega-3 fatty acids, B vitamins, and minerals like iron and zinc are crucial for cognitive functions and brain health.

- ⇨ **Immune System:**
  Vitamins A, C, D, and minerals such as selenium and zinc strengthen immunity, helping children fight infections and diseases.

Diseases Related to Inadequate Diets

Modern dietary habits can lead to numerous health problems in children:

- ➢ ***Obesity:***
  Excessive consumption of calories, sugars, and trans fats leads to overweight and obesity, increasing the risk of type 2 diabetes, heart disease, and other health issues.

- ➢ ***Vitamin and Mineral Deficiencies:***
  A diet low in fresh fruits, vegetables, whole grains, and proteins

can lead to nutrient deficiencies, adversely affecting physical and mental development.

- ***Chronic Diseases:***
  Poor diet can contribute to the development of chronic diseases, such as asthma, allergies, and even some cancers.

How to Improve Children's Diet Quality

As parents and caregivers, there are several steps you can take to improve your children's diet quality:

- **Water:**
  Water is very important even for infants, especially when introducing solid foods into their diet. It not only quenches thirst but also hydrates the body effectively. Children weighing up to 10 kg need 100 ml of fluids per kilogram of body weight. Children weighing over 10 kg should drink about 1000 ml of fluids daily, plus 50 ml for each kilogram over 10 kg.

- **Introducing Healthy Eating Habits:**
  Encouraging children to eat fresh fruits, vegetables, whole grains, and lean proteins.

- **Limiting Processed Foods:**
  Avoiding fast food, sweets, and sugary drinks in favor of healthier alternatives.

- **Nutritional Education:**
  Teaching children about the value of healthy foods and the impact of diet on their health and well-being.

⇨ **Cooking Together:**
Involving children in meal preparation, which can increase their interest in healthy eating.

Short Summary - My Daily Life

Healthy eating for children is the foundation of their proper development and overall health. By introducing healthy eating habits, educating children about the value of nutritious food, and avoiding processed foods, we can significantly improve the quality of life for the youngest. Unfortunately, in today's world, children's diets often rely on processed foods, sweets, and colorful drinks, leading to disrupted gut flora and frequent illnesses. Remember that eating habits are formed from the earliest years, even from birth. What children eat during their childhood impacts their entire lives. Childhood is the most crucial period for the development of the body. In my daily life, I encourage the youngest to drink water and experiment with healthy snacks and meals.

A Healthy and Sweet Breakfast Idea:

Recipe: Pancakes with Almond Butter and Blueberries

Ingredients: For the pancakes:

- 1 cup gluten-free flour
- 1 cup plant-based milk (e.g., almond, coconut)
- 2 eggs
- 1 tablespoon olive oil or vegetable oil
- A pinch of salt
- 1 tablespoon erythritol (optional)

For the filling:

- 4 tablespoons almond butter
- 1 cup blueberries
- 1 tablespoon honey or maple syrup (optional)

Preparation:

1. **Preparing the Pancakes:**
   - In a large bowl, mix the gluten-free flour, plant-based milk, eggs, olive oil, salt, and erythritol (if using). Stir until a smooth, lump-free batter forms.
   - Heat a non-stick skillet over medium heat. Add a little oil if necessary.
   - Pour a thin layer of batter onto the skillet, spreading it evenly by tilting the pan.
   - Cook the pancakes for about 2-3 minutes on each side until they are lightly golden.
   - Repeat until all the batter is used, placing the cooked pancakes on a plate.

2. **Preparing the Filling:**
   - Spread 1 tablespoon of almond butter evenly over each pancake.
   - Add a few blueberries on top of the almond butter.
   - Roll up the pancakes or fold them into triangles.

3. **Serving:**
   - Arrange the pancakes on a plate.
   - Drizzle with honey or maple syrup if desired.
   - Sprinkle with extra blueberries.

We've already discussed the challenges associated with modern dietary habits for children, including the negative impacts of consuming processed foods and excess sugar.

Another significant health threat is the presence of parasites in food, which can be an invisible yet serious issue. These parasites can lead to various diseases, making it crucial to understand how we can protect ourselves and our children from them. Let's now delve into a detailed analysis of this topic.

CHAPTER 27

Parasites in Food - An Invisible Threat to Health

Parasites in food are a threat that is often underestimated but can have serious health consequences. Parasites can enter our bodies through the consumption of contaminated food or water, and their presence can lead to various diseases. Understanding how parasites get into our food, what diseases they can cause, and how we can protect ourselves from them is crucial for maintaining health.

How Do Parasites Get Into Food?

Parasites can enter food in various ways:

- **Contaminated Water:**
  Parasites such as Cryptosporidium and Giardia are often found in contaminated water. Consuming unboiled or improperly filtered water can lead to infection.

- **Contaminated Vegetables and Fruits:**
  Plants grown in contaminated soil or watered with contaminated water can contain parasite eggs. Inadequately washing raw

vegetables and fruits before consumption increases the risk of infection.

- **Undercooked Meat:**
  Meat, especially pork, beef, and fish, can be infected with parasites like tapeworms or Trichinella. Consuming raw or undercooked meat can lead to infection.

- **Poor Hygiene:**
  Not following basic hygiene practices, such as washing hands before preparing and eating meals, can increase the risk of transferring parasites.

What Symptoms May Indicate a Parasitic Infection?

Parasites can inhabit various organs and cause different symptoms depending on their location. They most commonly reside in the digestive tract, particularly the intestines, liver, and pancreas, but can also affect the skin, lungs, muscles, reproductive organs, and brain. Common parasites found in humans include pinworms, human whipworms, roundworms, Giardia, tapeworms, and certain flukes.

Unfortunately, parasites can cause significant damage to the human body, leading to the development of many diseases. Due to the diversity of parasites and their potential habitats, the symptoms are often nonspecific and can be mistaken for other medical conditions. This is why many parasitic infections go undiagnosed for a long time.

Common Symptoms of Parasitic Infection

- **Nausea:** This can manifest as a persistent feeling of nausea, often intensifying after meals.

- **Abdominal Pain:** Regular stomach pain may indicate the presence of parasites in the intestines, leading to irritation and inflammation.
- **Bloating, Diarrhea, or Constipation:** Parasitic infections frequently disrupt normal digestive function, causing bloating, alternating diarrhea, and constipation.
- **Anemia:** Parasites can feed on the host's blood, leading to iron deficiency and, consequently, anemia.
- **Weight Loss:** Unexplained weight loss may occur as parasites absorb nutrients from food before the body can utilize them.
- **Skin Rash:** The presence of parasites can trigger allergic reactions, resulting in rashes and other skin issues.
- **Acne:** Parasitic infections can disturb the skin microbiome balance, contributing to acne development.
- **Chronic Fatigue:** A body infected with parasites often experiences chronic fatigue due to nutrient deficiencies and a weakened immune system.
- **Migraines:** Toxins released by parasites can affect the nervous system, causing recurring headaches and migraines.
- **Teeth Grinding:** Known as bruxism, teeth grinding, especially at night, can be a stress response to the presence of parasites.
- **Allergies:** Parasites can increase sensitivity to allergens, leading to various allergic reactions.
- **Dark Circles Under the Eyes:** Chronic parasitic infections can cause fatigue and sleep disturbances, often resulting in dark circles under the eyes.

Parasites - Psychological Symptoms

Parasites can cause a range of psychological symptoms that are often not directly associated with parasitic infections. Here are some possible signs that parasites may be affecting the nervous system:

- **Apathy**: Lack of energy and motivation to engage in activities.
- **Insomnia and Sleep Disorders**: Difficulty falling asleep and maintaining continuous sleep.
- **Depression**: Feelings of deep sadness, hopelessness, and a lack of interest in life.
- **Hyperactivity in Children**: Increased physical activity and difficulty focusing attention.
- **Neurosis**: A state of anxiety, irritability, and tension.
- **Anxiety**: A continuous feeling of worry and fear.
- **Memory Problems**: Difficulty in remembering and recalling information.
- **Irritability**: Easily angered and irritable.
- **Mental Fog**: Problems with concentration and thinking clearly.

Parasites in the Body - Symptoms in Children

Parasites can cause numerous symptoms in children that may be mistaken for other conditions. In addition to allergies, parasites can lead to chronic immune system issues. Symptoms may include:

- **Chronic Rhinitis**: Persistent nasal discharge down the back of the throat.
- **Weakness and Chronic Fatigue**: Loss of energy and a feeling of constant tiredness.
- **Recurrent Sinus Infections**: Frequent sinus problems.

- **Prolonged Cough without Infectious Cause**: A cough with no clear infectious reason.
- **Numerous Viral Infections**: Frequent viral infections.
- **Muscle and Joint Pain**: Pain not related to strain or intense physical activity.
- **Deterioration of Hearing or Vision**: Problems with hearing and vision.
- **Teeth Grinding**: Nighttime grinding of teeth.

If these symptoms are present, it is advisable to consider testing for parasites and initiating deworming treatment.

Diseases Caused by Parasites

According to available data, there are approximately 300 species of human parasites. Parasitic diseases can be caused by protozoa, nematodes, flatworms, and arthropods, which are most often external parasites.

The development of parasitosis can occur not only through the invasion of the parasite itself but also through infection with its eggs or larvae.

Examples of parasitic diseases:

- ***Pinworm infection:***
  Caused by Enterobius vermicularis (pinworms). It manifests as itching around the anus, sleep disturbances, fatigue, irritability, abdominal pain, loss of appetite, and teeth grinding.

- ***Human louse (Pediculus humanus):***
  The human louse (Pediculus humanus) is a parasite responsible for pediculosis, which easily spreads through direct contact with

an infected person or by using the same personal items such as combs, clothing, or towels. Symptoms of pediculosis include intense itching of the scalp and body. Scratching the bite areas can lead to sores that may become infected with bacteria. Lice can also transmit serious diseases, such as typhus. Pediculosis is particularly common in large groups of people, especially among children and adolescents attending nurseries, kindergartens, and schools.

- ***Human itch mite (Sarcoptes scabiei):***
  The human itch mite (Sarcoptes scabiei) is a parasitic mite that causes scabies. This disease manifests as skin lesions in the form of scales, blisters, and burrows, often covered with yellow-brown crusts. The infected person experiences intense itching, which worsens after the skin is warmed. The itch mite is a cosmopolitan parasite, meaning it occurs worldwide and can be transmitted through direct contact with an infected person.

- ***Fleas (Ctenocephalides canis):***
  Fleas, specifically the species Ctenocephalides canis, are parasitic insects that feed on the blood of their hosts, including humans. Their bites are not only bothersome, causing intense itching and discomfort, but can also trigger allergic reactions. Fleas are also known to be vectors for other parasites, such as the dog tapeworm (Dipylidium caninum). Infection with this tapeworm can occur accidentally, for example, through swallowing an infected flea.

- ***Giardiasis (lambliosis):***
  Caused by the parasite Giardia lamblia, which contaminates water and food. It manifests as diarrhea, abdominal pain, nausea, and

vomiting. Digestive and absorption disorders are observed, which can lead to malnutrition and body weakening.

- ***Toxoplasmosis:***
  This disease is caused by the protozoan Toxoplasma gondii, which lodges inside the cells of various human tissues. The main symptoms include fever, headaches, symptoms of pneumonia and myocarditis, lymph node enlargement, spleen and liver enlargement, and inflammation of the meninges and brain.

- ***Ascariasis:***
  Ascariasis is a disease caused by the human roundworm (Ascaris lumbricoides), which is one of the most common parasites in humans worldwide. This parasite, which resides in the small intestine, can also damage other organs, such as the liver and lungs, due to its life cycle. Typical symptoms of ascariasis include skin itching, hives, swelling of the face and hands, coughing, watery eyes, sleep disturbances, and hyperactivity. In advanced cases, more severe symptoms related to internal organ damage may also occur.

- ***Tapeworm Infections:***
  Tapeworms, such as Taenia saginata (beef tapeworm) and Taenia solium (pork tapeworm), can infect humans through the consumption of undercooked meat. Symptoms may include abdominal pain, weight loss, digestive problems, and other severe gastrointestinal issues. Concerning symptoms include apathy and weakness, vomiting, headaches, vision disturbances, and memory problems.

- ***Echinococcosis:***

  Echinococcosis is a disease caused by Echinococcus granulosus (hydatid tapeworm) and Echinococcus multilocularis (alveolar tapeworm). These tapeworms are most commonly found in dogs, foxes, and wolves, but their larvae increasingly infect humans as well. After ingesting the parasite's eggs, the larvae can lodge in various organs, most commonly the liver, and less frequently the lungs and brain. The presence of larvae in the body poses a serious, often fatal threat, as they cause the formation of hydatid cysts that can grow for years. One of the major problems with echinococcosis is the long incubation period – it can take several years from infection to the appearance of symptoms, which makes diagnosis and treatment challenging.

- ***Trichinosis (trichinellosis):***

  Trichinosis, also known as trichinellosis, is a disease caused by the parasitic worm Trichinella spiralis. Infection occurs through the consumption of undercooked or raw meat containing the larvae of the parasite. Trichinosis is not transmitted from person to person. Mature Trichinella worms live in the small intestine, where females give birth to larvae. These larvae travel through the bloodstream to the muscles, where they encyst, forming cysts that can calcify over time. Symptoms of trichinosis include fever, abdominal pain, diarrhea, muscle pain, allergic skin reactions, and facial swelling due to an allergic reaction.

- ***Cryptosporidiosis:***

  Cryptosporidiosis is a disease caused by Cryptosporidium, a parasite found in contaminated water. The parasite causes inflammation of the intestines, stomach, and sometimes the throat. It is characterized by short-term diarrhea, malaise, fever, nausea, vomiting, and abdominal pain.

Candida Overgrowth

When considering the topic of parasites, it is important to mention Candida, specifically its overgrowth. Our gastrointestinal tract hosts not only bacteria but also yeast-like fungi of the genus Candida, the most common of which is Candida albicans. Up to 90% of people have these fungi as part of their normal gut flora, and 25-50% of healthy individuals are carriers of Candida spp. in the oral cavity. Gastrointestinal candidiasis, which is the pathological overgrowth of Candida fungi, is an opportunistic infection that is becoming a serious issue in society. Infection most commonly occurs when the body's immunity is weakened, for example, after antibiotic therapy, which destroys some of the "good" bacteria in the intestines, allowing fungi to proliferate. An inappropriate diet, rich in simple sugars such as sweets, dried fruits, sweetened beverages, and juices, also promotes their growth. Fungal infections of the gastrointestinal tract often affect individuals with immune disorders, such as patients undergoing immunosuppression, those with hematologic diseases, and children with neurodevelopmental disorders, such as autism spectrum disorder.

The most common symptoms of Candida overgrowth in the gastrointestinal tract include:

- **Mucosal infections**: thrush that can occur in the mouth and affect the digestive system.
- **Localized skin infections**: vesicular lesions, known as intertrigo, in moist areas such as the groin or armpits.
- **Nervous system symptoms**: memory disorders, chronic fatigue syndrome, hyperactivity, anxiety, and panic attacks.

- **Gastrointestinal symptoms**: abdominal pain, constipation, digestive disorders, and heartburn.

Gastrointestinal candidiasis can affect the entire body, making it sometimes very difficult to identify the source of the problem.

How to Protect Yourself from Parasites in Food

There are several key steps you can take to protect yourself from parasites in food:

⇨ **Thoroughly Washing Fruits and Vegetables:**
Washing raw fruits and vegetables under running water helps remove parasites and other contaminants.

⇨ **Cooking Meat Properly:**
Ensure meat is thoroughly cooked. Check that it has reached a safe internal temperature that will kill any parasites.

⇨ **Avoiding Raw Meat and Fish:**
Eating raw meat and fish, such as in sushi or tartare, carries the risk of parasitic infection.

⇨ **Boiling Water:**
If you are unsure about the quality of the water, boil it before consumption. Boiling water effectively eliminates most parasites.

⇨ **Maintaining Good Hygiene:**
Regular handwashing, especially before eating and after using the restroom, helps reduce the risk of transferring parasites.

Anti-Parasitic Diet

Enhancing your daily diet with ingredients that support the fight against parasites can significantly aid the natural cleansing processes of the body. Such products include: garlic, beet juice and beet kvass, sauerkraut or pickle juice, kombucha, oregano oil, and spices like ginger, horseradish, thyme, fennel, and cayenne pepper.

Basic Principles of an Anti-Parasitic Diet:

⇨ **Fiber-Rich Foods:**
Consuming a large amount of vegetables, fruits, and whole grain products helps eliminate parasites from the body.

⇨ **Avoiding Sugar, Milk, and Wheat:**
During a deworming treatment, it is recommended to exclude these products from the diet as they can promote the growth of parasites.

⇨ **Regular Consumption of Garlic:**
Garlic has strong anti-parasitic and antibacterial properties. It can be added to dishes or consumed raw.

⇨ **Regular Consumption of Pumpkin Seeds:**
Pumpkin seeds are rich in substances that paralyze parasites, making it easier to remove them from the body.

⇨ **Probiotics:**
Fermented products such as natural yogurt, kefir, sauerkraut, and kombucha support a healthy gut microbiome, which helps fight parasites.

Home Remedies for Parasites

A highly effective and natural way to remove parasites from the body is through phytotherapy. This branch of medicine, also known as herbal medicine, uses plants for the treatment and prevention of diseases and has scientifically proven therapeutic, including deworming, effects. Herbal and homeopathic treatments can be used both for confirmed parasitic infections and as a preventive measure. It is believed that such treatments are best conducted cyclically, for example, twice a year in spring and autumn, under the supervision of a naturopath, homeopath, or other competent professional.

Plants particularly effective in anti-parasitic therapies include:

✓ **Wormwood:**
Has antihelminthic, antiseptic properties and supports metabolism. It is important to adhere to the recommended daily dosage.

✓ **Tansy:**
Combats pinworms, roundworms, and mites. It also has antibacterial, antifungal, and antiviral properties.

✓ **Pumpkin Seeds:**
Effective against intestinal parasites, especially tapeworms.

✓ **Cloves:**
Exhibit strong anti-parasitic properties and regulate stomach contractions.

✓ **Green and Black Walnut:**
Act as antidiarrheals and regulate the digestive system, effective against roundworms.

- ✓ **Black Cumin (Nigella Sativa):**
  Fights pinworms, tapeworms, Trichinella spiralis, and certain flukes.

- ✓ **Walnuts:**
  Effective against pinworms and roundworms.

In addition to the treatment, it is beneficial to enrich the daily diet with ingredients that aid in fighting parasites. Avoid the following: dairy products, sweets (except a small amount of honey), white flour, white rice, yeast, fried foods, red meat, monosodium glutamate, processed foods, especially store-bought ready meals, deli meats, mayonnaise, and ketchup (unless homemade from organic tomatoes), fast food, stimulants (coffee), and alcohol.

During deworming, it is also important to maintain strict hygiene, frequently changing bed linens, which along with personal underwear, should be ironed during this period. Remember that if one household member has a problem with parasites, all members should undergo deworming treatment, even if they do not show symptoms. Exceptions include pregnant and breastfeeding women, as well as individuals weakened by other illnesses. Simultaneously, if you have pets, they should also be dewormed (dogs, hamsters, parrots, cats).

During preparation for deworming, I recommend detoxifying the body. If parasites are present in our body, there are also large amounts of toxins, viruses, bacteria, and fungi. Drinking plenty of water is fundamental to continuously cleanse the body.

Always carry out deworming treatment under the supervision of a competent person, such as a doctor, homeopath, or naturopath.

Short Summary - My Daily Life

The issue of parasitic infections is often underestimated and overlooked in medicine. There is insufficient education on this topic, and the damage parasites can cause to our bodies is serious. Parasites in food pose a significant yet often underappreciated threat to health. They can cause a wide range of ailments, from digestive issues to severe systemic diseases.

We deworm our pets but forget about ourselves. Parasites can lead to a series of serious health problems, both physical and psychological. Understanding how parasites enter our food and the symptoms they can cause is crucial for maintaining health. By adhering to hygiene principles, thoroughly washing food, properly cooking meat, and using natural treatment methods, we can significantly reduce the risk of parasitic infections and enjoy a healthier life. If we notice concerning symptoms, we can consider an anti-parasitic diet and consult a competent professional for deworming. In my daily diet, I regularly include pumpkin seeds and black cumin oil. I have undergone deworming and detoxification processes multiple times, always feeling much better afterward.

While parasites in food can be an invisible yet serious threat, other modern health threats are more obvious but often ignored. Energy drinks, alcohol, and various stimulants have long been part of many people's culture and daily lives. Unfortunately, their widespread social acceptance does not align with awareness of the serious negative effects they can have on physical and mental health.

CHAPTER 28

Energy Drinks, Alcohol, and Stimulants - Subtle Killers of Our Health

In today's society, energy drinks, alcohol, and various stimulants are widely available and broadly accepted. While they may provide temporary benefits, their long-term consumption carries significant risks for both physical and mental health.

Energy Drinks

Consuming energy drinks in small quantities can beneficially stimulate the central nervous system. However, larger doses may lead to symptoms such as irritability, anxiety, panic attacks, insomnia, or motor coordination disorders. A concerning trend today is their consumption by teenagers.

Energy drinks contain high concentrations of caffeine, sugar, and other stimulants like taurine, guarana, and B vitamins. They are designed to increase energy levels, improve concentration, and enhance physical performance.

Regular consumption of energy drinks can lead to serious health issues, particularly heart problems. High doses of caffeine can cause heart rhythm disorders, hypertension, and in extreme cases, heart attacks. As mentioned earlier, excessive caffeine can disrupt sleep patterns, leading to insomnia, chronic fatigue, and concentration problems. After the initial "energy boost," users may experience concentration issues and fatigue. Additionally, these drinks can affect metabolic balance. The high sugar content can lead to obesity, type 2 diabetes, and other metabolic disorders.

Alcohol

Consuming alcohol negatively impacts numerous systems in the human body, with the nervous system being particularly sensitive to any substances. Frequent alcohol consumption leads to brain shrinkage by eliminating neuron connections and causing neuron death. Alcohol consumption can lead to numerous health issues. While some studies suggest that moderate alcohol consumption may have certain health benefits, excessive drinking is undeniably harmful and causes liver diseases.

Alcohol is a leading cause of cirrhosis and other liver diseases. Regular alcohol consumption damages liver cells, leading to fatty liver, hepatitis, and cirrhosis.

Alcohol can lead to hypertension, heart disease, and increase the risk of stroke and cancers. Alcohol consumption raises the risk of liver cancer, breast cancer, colorectal cancer, esophageal cancer, throat cancer, and oral cancer.

E-Cigarettes

Electric cigarettes, also known as e-cigarettes, have gained popularity as an alternative to traditional cigarettes, but they bring new health risks. Although often marketed as less harmful, e-cigarettes can lead to serious health problems. Studies have shown that their use is associated with the risk of lung damage, cardiovascular disease, and respiratory issues. E-cigarettes contain chemical substances such as nicotine, diacetyl, and heavy metals, which can be toxic. Long-term inhalation of these substances can lead to chronic diseases and addiction, particularly among young people who are more susceptible to the effects of nicotine addiction.

Nicotine

Nicotine causes the narrowing of blood vessels and impairs blood flow to the skin, which then does not receive enough oxygen and vitamins. This blocks the regeneration process, causing the skin to lose its ability to retain water and become wrinkled. Nicotine, the primary active ingredient in tobacco, leads to strong addiction. Smoking tobacco has numerous negative health effects, such as lung cancer, heart disease, and chronic respiratory diseases. Smokers often suffer from chronic bronchitis and chronic obstructive pulmonary disease (COPD).

Drugs

Drugs have a profound impact on the brain and body, often leading to addiction. Drug addiction is a serious health issue that can lead to numerous negative consequences. Drugs like cocaine, amphetamine, heroin, and other "designer drugs" can cause permanent brain damage.

They can also lead to heart problems, including hypertension, arrhythmias, and even heart attacks.

Impact on the Digestive and Immune Systems

- ***Energy Drinks:***
  The high caffeine and sugar content can cause digestive disorders, such as ulcers and acid reflux. Excess sugar and caffeine can weaken the immune response, increasing the risk of infections and chronic diseases.

- ***Alcohol:***
  It can cause gastritis, stomach ulcers, and issues with the pancreas, such as pancreatitis. Excessive alcohol consumption weakens the immune system, increasing susceptibility to infections.

- ***E-cigarettes:***
  E-cigarettes, though marketed as a safer alternative to traditional cigarettes, can negatively affect the digestive and immune systems. The nicotine in e-cigarettes irritates the stomach lining, leading to gastritis, peptic ulcers, and reflux. The chemicals in e-cigarettes disrupt the gut microbiome, which can result in digestive problems and impaired nutrient absorption. Additionally, toxins from e-cigarettes weaken the function of immune cells, increasing the risk of infections.

- ***Nicotine:***
  Smoking negatively affects the function of the esophagus, stomach, and intestines, increasing the risk of gastroesophageal reflux disease (GERD) and inflammatory bowel diseases. Smoking

also diminishes the body's ability to fight infections by impairing white blood cell function.

- ***Drugs:***
  Drugs have a negative impact on the digestive and immune systems. Regular use of psychoactive substances can lead to stomach problems such as nausea, vomiting, abdominal pain, and diarrhea. They damage the stomach lining, which can cause ulcers and inflammation. Additionally, drugs weaken the immune system, increasing susceptibility to infections, viral, and bacterial diseases.

Impact on Mental Health

- ***Energy Drinks:***
  Energy drinks contain high doses of caffeine and other stimulants, which can lead to excessive stimulation, insomnia, nervousness, and anxiety attacks. Prolonged consumption of energy drinks can cause heart rhythm disorders, impacting mental health by increasing stress levels. Excessive intake of these drinks, especially when combined with alcohol, poses a serious threat to both mental and physical health.

- ***Alcohol:***
  Consuming alcohol, especially in large quantities, can have serious effects on mental health. Alcohol acts as a depressant on the central nervous system, which can lead to mood deterioration, anxiety, and the intensification of depression symptoms. Excessive alcohol consumption can also cause memory problems, concentration issues, and sleep disturbances. Long-term alcohol

abuse increases the risk of developing alcoholism, which has a destructive impact on mental and emotional health.

- ***E-cigarettes and Nicotine:***
  Nicotine, found in both traditional cigarettes and e-cigarettes, acts as a stimulant on the central nervous system. Although it may temporarily improve mood and concentration, long-term use leads to addiction, which increases levels of stress and anxiety. Individuals addicted to nicotine are more prone to developing depressive and anxiety disorders. Additionally, e-cigarettes, often perceived as less harmful, can contain harmful chemicals that may negatively impact mental health.

- ***Drugs:***
  Drugs, depending on the type, can have various and often very harmful effects on mental health. For example, amphetamines and cocaine act as stimulants, which can lead to paranoia, hallucinations, and mood disorders. Regular drug use leads to addiction, significantly lowering quality of life and mental health. Drugs affect neurotransmitter levels such as serotonin and dopamine. In the initial phase of drug use, there may be a rapid increase in these substances, leading to feelings of euphoria. However, over time, regular use depletes the brain's serotonin and dopamine reserves, resulting in depressive states, anhedonia (inability to feel pleasure), and chronic fatigue. This neurotransmitter deficit can lead to serious mental disorders that require long-term treatment.

Short Summary - My Daily Life

In life, we encounter numerous occasions, such as gatherings with friends or family parties, where alcohol is often present. We are all human, and it's not about completely abstaining from alcohol. It also has some health benefits. A glass of red wine effectively enhances appetite and stimulates the secretion of digestive juices. Moreover, red wine helps digest fatty foods, improves brain function, memory, and concentration, and reduces the risk of Alzheimer's disease. On the other hand, a small glass of good cognac is recommended for people with circulation problems, as it speeds up the heartbeat, lowers blood pressure, improves circulation, activates organ functions, and simultaneously alleviates stress. The key aspect is moderation and choosing the lesser evil. Regular consumption of beer or a glass of sweet wine every day is very harmful to our body. This way, we burden the liver, pancreas, and the entire body. Interestingly, our liver metabolizes high-proof spirits better, so a better choice would be clear spirits like vodka, served with ice cubes and lemon. Conversely, the worst choice would be combining them with high-sugar juices or carbonated drinks and making cocktails.

Health threats to our bodies appear every day, so awareness in making decisions while enjoying life is essential.

Balance is the key to success – let's not get carried away, but remember to exercise common sense.

PART X

BODY CLEANSING

CHAPTER 29

Why Detoxification is Necessary in Today's World

Our bodies are exposed to significantly more toxins than ever before. Air pollution, chemicals in food, preservatives, pesticides, heavy metals, and environmental contaminants are just some of the factors that can burden our system. As a result, more and more people are turning to detoxification as a way to improve their health and well-being. In this chapter, we will examine why body detoxification is important, how it works, and what detox methods can be effective.

Modern Sources of Toxins

Modern life exposes us to various sources of toxins that can burden our bodies:

- **Air Pollution:**
  Car exhaust, industrial emissions, and cigarette smoke are major sources of air pollution that we inhale daily.

- **Chemicals in Food:**
  Pesticides, herbicides, preservatives, and artificial additives are commonly used in food production.

- **Heavy Metals:**
  Mercury, lead, cadmium, and arsenic can enter the body through contaminated food, water, and air.

- **Everyday Products:**
  Cosmetics, cleaning products, and other household items may contain harmful chemicals.

Why is Detox Needed?

The human body has natural detoxification mechanisms, primarily through the liver, kidneys, skin, and lungs. However, excessive toxin overload can overwhelm these systems, leading to the accumulation of harmful substances and a decline in health. Here are a few reasons why detox is important:

⇨ **Strengthening the Immune System:**
Detoxification helps remove toxins that can weaken the immune system and increase susceptibility to infections.

⇨ **Improving Digestion:**
Eliminating toxins from the digestive system can enhance digestion and nutrient absorption.

⇨ **Increasing Energy:**
A cleansed body functions better, which can lead to increased energy levels and overall well-being.

⇨ **Better Skin:**
Detoxification can improve skin appearance, reducing acne, rashes, and other skin issues.

⇨ **Reducing Inflammation:**
Removing toxins can reduce inflammation, which is the root cause of many chronic diseases.

Detox Methods

There are many detoxification methods that can support the body's natural cleansing processes:

✓ **Dietary Detox:**
Consuming foods rich in fiber, antioxidants, and nutrients can aid detoxification processes. Key elements of such a diet include fruits, vegetables, whole grains, and healthy fats.

✓ **Juice Cleanses:**
Juice cleanses can give the digestive system a break and allow it to regenerate while providing the body with essential vitamins and minerals.

✓ **Short Fasts and Fasting:**
Short-term fasts can relieve the body. Fasting, practiced for thousands of years in traditional medicine, has cleansing, regenerative, and strengthening effects on the body. Water or juice fasting, using organic fruits and vegetables, is an ideal way to maintain health throughout life. During fasts, your body detoxifies by eliminating accumulated toxins from cells, which can alleviate or reduce the severity of conditions such as allergies, migraines, digestive problems, and many others.

- ✓ **Colon Hydrotherapy:**
  Treatments like colon hydrotherapy can help remove accumulated toxins from the intestines.

- ✓ **Physical Exercise:**
  Regular physical activity boosts circulation and speeds up the elimination of toxins through sweat and exhaled air.

- ✓ **Saunas and Detox Baths:**
  Baths with Epsom salts, steam saunas, and dry saunas can support the sweating process, which helps remove toxins through the skin.

- ✓ **Supplements and Herbs:**
  Certain supplements and herbs can support the liver and other organs in the detoxification process.

Supplements and Herbs Supporting Detoxification

Detoxification is a key process for maintaining overall health, as it helps the body eliminate toxins and harmful substances. Certain supplements and herbs can support this process by aiding the liver and other organs in their natural detoxifying functions. Here are some examples of supplements and herbs known for their detoxifying properties, highlighting their benefits.

- ✓ **Milk Thistle:**
  Milk thistle contains silymarin, a powerful antioxidant that aids in liver cell regeneration. It is particularly effective in protecting the liver from toxins, making it a popular supplement in detox processes.

- ✓ **Chlorella:**

  Chlorella pyrenoidosa is a green algae known for its detoxifying properties, especially in binding and removing heavy metals from the body. Scientific studies have shown that this algae absorbs heavy metals and other toxic substances from the intestines and expels them naturally from the body.

- ✓ **Spirulina:**

  Spirulina is another algae rich in protein, vitamins, and minerals. It has antioxidant and anti-inflammatory properties, supporting detoxification processes in the body. Spirulina is also known for its blood-cleansing properties.

- ✓ **Dandelion Root:**

  Dandelion root is a natural diuretic, which helps remove toxins through urine. It is also used to support liver function and the digestive system.

- ✓ **Nettle:**

  Nettle has blood-cleansing properties and helps remove excess fluids from the body, making it useful in detox processes. It is rich in vitamins and minerals that support overall health.

- ✓ **Cistus (Rock Rose):**

  Cistus is a strong antioxidant with anti-inflammatory effects. It helps cleanse the body of toxins, supports the immune system, and protects against infections.

- ✓ **Chlorophyll:**

  Chlorophyll is considered a superfood because of its antioxidant and anticancer properties. Chlorophyll can help detoxify the body by binding to toxins and preventing them from being absorbed elsewhere. Chlorophyll may also help the lymphatic system remove harmful toxins from the blood.

Detox Juices

Detox juices are not only delicious but also packed with ingredients that support the body's natural cleansing processes. These juices can be a great addition to your daily diet, helping to maintain health and well-being.

Benefits of Detox Juices:

- ⇨ **Rich in Nutrients:** Full of vitamins, minerals, and antioxidants.
- ⇨ **Improves Digestion:** Helps maintain a healthy digestive system.
- ⇨ **Boosts Energy:** Provides a natural energy boost.
- ⇨ **Enhances Immunity:** Strengthens the immune system.
- ⇨ **Promotes Clear Skin:** Improves skin health and appearance.

Tips for Making Detox Juices:

- ⇨ **Use Organic Produce:** To avoid pesticides and other harmful chemicals.
- ⇨ **Drink Fresh:** Consume juices immediately after preparation to preserve their nutrient content.
- ⇨ **Experiment:** Try different combinations of fruits and vegetables to find your favorite flavors.
- ⇨ **Add Superfoods:** Include ingredients like ginger, turmeric, and leafy greens for added health benefits.

Incorporating detox juices into your diet can help you feel rejuvenated and energized while supporting your body's natural detoxification processes.

Here are some examples:

Recipe: Detox Juice with Cucumber, Spinach, Apple, Lemon, and Ginger

Ingredients:

- 1 cucumber
- 1 cup spinach
- 1 apple
- 1 lemon (juiced)
- Small piece of ginger (about 2 cm)

- 1 cup water
- Ice (optional)

Preparation:

1. Thoroughly wash the cucumber, spinach, and apple.
2. Cut the cucumber and apple into smaller pieces.
3. Blend the cucumber, spinach, apple, lemon juice, and ginger with water until smooth.
4. Strain the juice through a sieve to remove the pulp (optional).
5. You can also make the juice using a slow juicer or a centrifugal juicer.
6. Serve the juice with ice if you prefer a more refreshing drink.

Recipe: Citrus Detox Juice

Ingredients:

- 2 oranges
- 1 grapefruit
- 1 lemon
- A handful of mint leaves

Instructions:

1. Peel the oranges, grapefruit, and lemon.
2. Cut them into segments.
3. Add all ingredients to a juicer and blend until smooth.
4. Garnish with mint leaves and serve.

Remember to choose organic products or buy from trusted local farmers to avoid harmful substances.

For more recipes, check out the book: ***"Sugar, Gluten, and Dairy-Free Recipes".***

Short Summary - My Daily Life

Let's turn our thoughts back to our home. Imagine what your home would look like if you didn't clean it for months or even years. Picture every corner and crevice. It seems unimaginable, right? We clean our homes at least once a week, and do thorough cleanings in the spring and winter. But what about our bodies? Just as dirt accumulates in our homes, toxins build up in our bodies—in the liver, intestines, and other organs. That's why we need to do regular cleanings, known as detox.

I detox twice a year to give my body a break. My journey began with completely eliminating sugar, followed by fruit and vegetable diets and juice fasts. After 10 years of practicing detoxification, I now practice water fasts, also known as therapeutic fasting. In between fasts, I try to include single juice days and longer intervals between meals. I use chlorella pyrenoidosa daily and also practice intermittent fasting (IF). This method involves not consuming foods or drinks containing calories for a specified period. After this period, there is an eating window during which meals can be consumed. The eating window can vary in length, but the most popular variant is an 8/16 split, which means an 8-hour eating window followed by a 16-hour fast, including sleep. Eating windows can be adjusted individually, for example, 10/14 or even 12/12 at the beginning.

Water is a fundamental element of the diet, and we often forget about it. We frequently confuse thirst with hunger. Water is crucial in detoxifying the body because it helps eliminate accumulated toxins from our system.

Another important aspect is physical activity. We lead sedentary lifestyles, but our bodies need movement. Regular physical activity strengthens and improves the respiratory and circulatory systems: it reduces the risk of cardiovascular diseases and helps prevent hypertension. It has been proven to decrease the occurrence of type 2 diabetes and some cancers. The World Health Organization recommends that healthy individuals take 6,000 to 8,000 steps daily. I adhere to this guideline, and my daily challenge is to take a minimum of 8,000 steps each day.

Detoxifying the body is an essential part of modern life, helping to reduce the buildup of toxins and improve overall health. By using appropriate detox methods, we can support the body's natural cleansing processes, strengthen the immune system, and enhance our well-being. Feeling light and full of energy is the goal.

CHAPTER 30

Mental Health - The Key to Well-being

In today's globalized and rapidly changing world, mental health is becoming an increasingly important aspect of our lives.

Every day, we spend a lot of time—sometimes too much—on our phones, laptops, and televisions, which can negatively impact our mental health. Excessive use of electronic devices can lead to sleep problems, increased stress levels, and social isolation. Understanding how to care for mental health and manage stress, anxiety, and other emotional issues is crucial for achieving a full and satisfying life. In this chapter, we will explore how diet, physical activity, sleep, and other factors affect our mental health, as well as strategies we can use to improve our well-being.

The Importance of Mental Health

Mental health encompasses our emotional, psychological, and social well-being. It affects how we think, feel, and act in our daily lives. It is crucial for managing stress, building interpersonal relationships, and making decisions.

The Impact of Diet on Mental Health

Diet plays a significant role in maintaining mental health. Proper nutrition can help manage stress, anxiety, and depression.

A key component is omega-3 fatty acids, found in fish, flaxseeds, and walnuts. These are crucial for brain health, helping to reduce inflammation and improve mood. B vitamins, present in whole grains, meat, and legumes, are essential for the production of neurotransmitters, which affect the functioning of the nervous system. Antioxidants, found in fruits like berries and vegetables such as spinach and carrots, protect the brain from oxidative stress, supporting its health and function.

Avoiding harmful ingredients is equally important. Excess sugar can lead to mood swings, fatigue, and anxiety. Processed foods containing preservatives, artificial colors, and trans fats can negatively affect mental health, making it advisable to avoid them in your daily diet.

Physical Activity and Mental Health

Regular physical activity has a positive impact on mental health. Exercise helps release endorphins, which improve mood, reduce stress, and alleviate anxiety. Aerobic exercises such as running, swimming, and cycling are excellent for improving mental health because they engage the entire body and increase overall fitness. Yoga is ideal for relaxation, stress reduction, and improved concentration by combining movement, breath, and meditation. Strength training enhances the body, boosts self-esteem, and builds confidence by developing strength and endurance. Incorporating various forms of physical activity into daily life can bring significant benefits for mental health and overall well-being.

Sleep and Mental Health

Good sleep is essential for mental health. Lack of sleep can lead to problems with concentration, memory, and an increased risk of depression and anxiety. To ensure healthy sleep, it is important to pay attention to a few key factors.

- ⇨ A regular sleep schedule is very important. Going to bed and waking up at the same time every day helps regulate the sleep cycle, promoting better sleep quality and overall well-being. A consistent daily rhythm helps the body function better.

- ⇨ Healthy pre-sleep habits also play a significant role. Avoiding caffeine and electronic devices before bedtime, as well as engaging in relaxing rituals like reading a book or taking a warm bath, can significantly improve sleep quality.

Creating an evening routine that helps you unwind and prepare your body for sleep is beneficial. By making these simple changes in your life, you can improve the quality of your sleep, which in turn will positively impact your mental health by enhancing concentration, improving memory, and reducing the risk of depression and anxiety.

Strategies for Coping with Stress

Stress is an inherent part of life, but appropriate coping strategies can help maintain mental health. Relaxation techniques, such as meditation, deep breathing, progressive muscle relaxation, and nature walks, are effective in reducing stress. Social support, through conversations with friends, family, or a therapist, can help manage difficult emotions and provide a sense of support and understanding. Finding time for healthy hobbies, such as reading, painting, or gardening, is also crucial for reducing stress and improving well-being.

By incorporating these strategies into your life, you can better manage stress, which will contribute to better mental health and overall well-being in the long run.

Short Summary - My Daily Life

A positive outlook on life is incredibly important. Starting with small changes and self-care can significantly improve our well-being. Every small improvement, like a healthy diet, regular physical activity, or a moment of relaxation, releases endorphins and makes us feel better about ourselves. Seeing the results of our efforts in the mirror boosts our self-esteem and makes us feel more valuable.

Mental and physical health are closely linked. Taking care of your body through healthy eating habits, regular exercise, and proper skincare brings both physical and emotional benefits. When we do something for ourselves, we invest in our well-being and health, which translates into better relationships with others and greater life satisfaction.

For example, regularly practicing mindfulness or meditation helps reduce stress and improve mood. Small changes like drinking more water, adding vegetables to meals, or taking a daily walk can bring significant health benefits.

It's important to remember that health is our most precious treasure, worth taking care of every day. A balanced approach to life, full of positive habits and mindful choices, leads to long-term well-being and a sense of fulfillment.

CONCLUSION

Health in Our Hands - Final Word

At the end of this journey through the complex world of nutrition and health, I want to emphasize one key thought: our health is in our hands. In the age of globalization, industrial agriculture, and the widespread availability of processed foods, making conscious dietary choices becomes not only a matter of individual health but also an act of social and ecological responsibility.

Education as a Foundation

Education and awareness are the foundations of a healthy lifestyle. By understanding how individual nutrients affect our bodies, we can make better choices about the foods we consume. Awareness of the dangers associated with pesticides, heavy metals, microplastics, and other contaminants allows us to take steps to protect our health and the health of our loved ones.

Conscious Choices

Conscious choices pertain not only to food but also to cosmetics, supplements, and other products we use daily. I would also like to mention the cookware we use for preparing our meals. Choosing cookware that does not release harmful substances during cooking and is durable—such as stainless steel, stone, enamel, and ceramic—can make a significant difference. Avoid cooking and reheating food in microwaves. Recent studies show that foods prepared in microwaves suffer molecular damage. Consuming such food can cause unnatural changes in human blood and immune systems.

By opting for natural, organic, and local products, we not only take care of our health but also support sustainable agricultural and production practices. Every purchase is a vote for a healthier and more sustainable world.

The Importance of Balance

Balance in diet and lifestyle is crucial. Proper hydration, balanced meals rich in diverse nutrients, regular physical activity, and mental health care are elements that collectively form the foundation of a healthy life. Let's not forget about detoxifying the body and maintaining gut microbiome health, which are integral parts of our well-being.

A Holistic Approach to Health

Health is not just the absence of disease but a state of complete physical, mental, and social well-being. A holistic approach to health considers all aspects of our lives, from diet and physical activity to emotional health. Understanding that each of these elements impacts our overall health allows us to take better care of ourselves and others.

Actions for the Future

Each of us can contribute to creating a healthier world for future generations. Making conscious dietary choices, supporting sustainable farming and production practices, and educating ourselves and others about health and the environment are steps that lead to positive change.

Gratitude and Commitment

In conclusion, I want to express my gratitude for taking this journey with me. I hope the information contained in this book helps you make more informed decisions and lead healthier, more fulfilling lives. Together, we can create a healthier, more sustainable world for all of us. Each of us can contribute to creating a healthier world for future generations. Making conscious dietary choices, supporting sustainable farming and production practices, and educating ourselves and others about health and the environment are steps that lead to positive changes.

Remember, your health is in your hands. Every step you take towards better health matters. Take care of your body, your home, and the vehicle that carries you through your life. Remember, a healthy body houses a healthy spirit!

Thank you for your trust and commitment. I wish you all the best on your journey to health and well-being.

Warm regards,
Joanna

BIBLIOGRAPHY

1. https://www.efsa.europa.eu/en/news/added-and-free-sugars-should-be-low-possible

2. https://www.ncbi.nlm.nih.gov/pmc/articles/PMC5793330/

3. National Center for Biotechnology Information. "Assessment of Pesticide Exposure." https://www.ncbi.nlm.nih.gov/pmc/articles/PMC4784299/

4. ScienceDirect. "Long-term health effects of glyphosate exposure." https://www.sciencedirect.com/science/article/pii/S0002916523135052

5. World Health Organization. "More than 3 billion people protected from harmful trans fat in their food." https://www.who.int/news-room/detail/09-09-2020-more-than-3-billion-people-protected-from-harmful-trans-fat-in-their-food

6. International Agency for Research on Cancer. "Glyphosate classified as a probable human carcinogen." https://www.iarc.who.int/featured-news/media-centre-iarc-news-glyphosate/

7. Giesey JP, Dobson S, Solomon KR. "Ecotoxicological risk assessment for roundup herbicide." Rev Environ Contam Toxicol. 2000;167:35–120.

8. Bates N, Campbell A. "Glyphosate." In: Campbell A, Campbell A, editors. Handbook of Poisoning in Dogs and Cat. 1st ed. England: Blackwell Science Ltd; 2000. pp. 135–8.

9. Sawada Y, Nagai Y, Ueyama M, Yamamoto I. "Probable toxicity of surface-active agent in commercial herbicide containing glyphosate." Lancet. 1988;1:299.

10. Comments to ANZFA about Applications A346, A362 and A363 from the Food Legislation and Regulation Advisory Group (FLRAG) of the Public Health Association of Australia (PHAA) on behalf of the PHAA, "Food produced from glyphosate-tolerant canola line GT73," http://www.iher.org.au/

11. "Long term toxicity of a Roundup herbicide and a Roundup-tolerant genetically modified maize," http://www.sciencedirect.com/science/article/pii/S0278691512005637

12. Netherwood et al. "Assessing the survival of transgenic plant DNA in the human gastrointestinal tract." Nature Biotechnology 22, 2004.

13. Townsend M. "Why soya is a hidden destroyer." Daily Express, March 1999.

14. World Health Organization. "Arsenic in drinking water." https://iris.who.int/bitstream/handle/10665/329482/WHO-CED-PHE-EPE-19.4.1-eng.pdf?ua=1#:~=A%20MAJOR%20PUBLIC%20HEALTH%20CONCERN,-Soluble%20inorganic%20arsenic&text=Human%20exposure%20to%20elevated%20levels,with%20high%2Darsenic%20water%20sources

15. World Health Organization. "Arsenic." https://www.who.int/news-room/fact-sheets/detail/arsenic

16. National Toxicology Program. "Cadmium." https://ntp.niehs.nih.gov/sites/default/files/ntp/roc/content/profiles/cadmium.pdf

17. World Health Organization. "Mercury and health." https://www.who.int/news-room/fact-sheets/detail/mercury-and-health

18. World Health Organization. "Lead poisoning and health." https://www.who.int/news-room/fact-sheets/detail/lead-poisoning-and-health

19. Sánchez-Villegas A, Toledo E, de Irala J, Ruiz-Canela M, Pla-Vidal J, Martínez-González MA. "Fast-food and commercial baked goods consumption and the risk of depression." Public Health Nutrition, 2011; 15 (03): 424. DOI: 10.1017/S1368980011001856

20. Medical News Today. "Health benefits of a balanced diet." https://www.medicalnewstoday.com/articles/324847

21. National Center for Biotechnology Information. "Obesity and mental health." https://www.ncbi.nlm.nih.gov/pmc/articles/PMC6146358/

22. Journal of Agricultural and Food Chemistry. "Removal of Surface Pesticide Residues on Produce by Washing with a Baking Soda Solution."

23. University of Tennessee. "Effectiveness of Vinegar for Removal of Foodborne Pathogens."

24. Brodowska AJ, Nowak A, Śmigielski K. "Ozone in the food industry: Principles of ozonation and its applications."

25. Khadre MA, Yousef AE, Kim JG. "Microbiological aspects of ozone applications in food: a review."

26. Tiwari BK, Brennan CS, Curran T, Gallagher E, Cullen PJ, O'Donnell CP. "Application of ozone in grain processing."

27. World Health Organization. "Obesity and overweight." https://www.who.int/news-room/fact-sheets/detail/obesity-and-overweight

28. PubMed. "Impact of diet on mental health." https://pubmed.ncbi.nlm.nih.gov/20819244/

29. Scientific Research Publishing. "The role of diet in mental health." https://www.scirp.org/reference/referencespapers?referenceid=2674881

30. Nature. "Obesity-related inflammation and mental health." https://www.nature.com/articles/s41598-020-71908-9

31. World Health Organization. "Cardiovascular diseases (CVDs)." https://www.who.int/news-room/fact-sheets/detail/cardiovascular-diseases-(cvds)

32. New York Times. "The science of healthy eating." https://www.nytimes.com/2006/10/17/health/17real.html

33. World Cancer Research Fund. "Summary of the Third Expert Report." https://www.wcrf.org/wp-content/uploads/2021/02/Summary-of-Third-Expert-Report-2018.pdf

34. National Center for Biotechnology Information. "Diet and Mental Health: Can What You Eat Affect How You Feel?" https://www.ncbi.nlm.nih.gov/pmc/articles/PMC5827298/

35. National Center for Biotechnology Information. "Nutritional psychiatry: Your brain on food." https://www.ncbi.nlm.nih.gov/pmc/articles/PMC5244028/

36. National Center for Biotechnology Information. "Impact of diet on mental health in adolescents." https://www.ncbi.nlm.nih.gov/pmc/articles/PMC8634384/

37. National Center for Biotechnology Information. "Omega-3 Fatty Acids: Health Benefits and Dietary Sources." https://ods.od.nih.gov/factsheets/Omega3FattyAcids-HealthProfessional/

38. PubMed. "The effect of omega-3 fatty acids on mental health." https://pubmed.ncbi.nlm.nih.gov/31383846/

39. PubMed. "Dietary patterns and depression risk: A meta-analysis." https://pubmed.ncbi.nlm.nih.gov/17061840/

40. National Center for Biotechnology Information. "Mental health benefits of dietary fiber." https://www.ncbi.nlm.nih.gov/pmc/articles/PMC4006993/

41. National Center for Biotechnology Information. "Dietary antioxidants and mental health: A review." https://www.ncbi.nlm.nih.gov/pmc/articles/PMC10384867/

42. National Center for Biotechnology Information. "The gut-brain axis and mental health." https://www.ncbi.nlm.nih.gov/pmc/articles/PMC6320968/

43. EBioMedicine. "Dietary fiber intake and depressive symptoms." https://www.ebiomedicine.com/article/S2352-3964(17)30233-5/fulltext

Printed in Great Britain
by Amazon

60798310R00161